Walk in the Light Series

The
Sabbath

Scriptural Truth Concerning the Sabbath
and Christian Sunday Observance

Todd D. Bennett

Strawberry Islands
Messianic Publishing
2303 Watterson Trail
Louisville, Ky 40299
502-261-9833

Shema Yisrael Publications

The Sabbath
Scriptural Truth Concerning the Sabbath and Christian Sunday
Observance

First printing 2005

ISBN: 0-9768659-1-2
Library of Congress Number: 2005906540

Cover design by Yeshai and Eliyahna Van Kuren

Printed in the United States of America.

Please visit our website for other titles:
www.shemayisrael.net

For information regarding publicity for author interviews call
(866) 866-2211

The
Sabbath

Scriptural Truth Concerning the Sabbath and Christian Sunday Observance

"There remains a Sabbath-keeping to the people of YHWH."
Hebrews 4:9

Table of Contents

Acknowledgments

I must first and foremost acknowledge my Creator, Redeemer and Savior who opened my eyes and showed me the Light. He never gave up on me even when, at times, it seemed that I gave up on Him. He is ever patient and truly awesome. His blessings, mercies and love endure forever and my gratitude and thanksgiving cannot be fully expressed in words.

Were it not for the patience, prayers, love and support of my beautiful wife Janet and my extraordinary daughter Morgan I would never have been able to accomplish this work. They gave me the freedom to pursue the vision and dreams that my Heavenly Father placed within me and for that I am so very grateful. I love them both more than they will ever know.

Loving thanks to my father who tirelessly watched and held down "the fort" while I was away traveling, researching and writing.

Special thanks to Yeshai Van Kuren and his wife, Eliyahna, for their superb creative assistance in the cover design and layout. I would also like to thank my friends in eretz Israel, Michael Rood and Bob Fischer, for their inspiration, assistance and encouragement. My appreciation to Rabbi Steven Galilee of Beit Shalom Synagogue for his support and candid comments as well as his wife Deborah for her invaluable Hebrew lessons.

Introduction

"²⁰ Everyone who does evil hates the light, and will not come into the light for fear that his deeds will be exposed. ²¹ But whoever lives by the truth comes into the light, so that it may be seen plainly that what he has done has been done through God."
John 3:20-21 NIV

This book entitled "The Sabbath" is part of a larger body of educational work called the "Walk in the Light" series. As such it is built upon a number of other topics and ideally the reader would have been briefed on such topics as Paganism, The Name of the Creator, The Scriptures, The Redeemed, The Redeemer and The Law and Grace among others. Due to the importance of the subject of this text, and each volume of the series, I have attempted to present them in such a fashion that they can stand alone. In order to do this I have used extensive annotations and I would encourage the reader to review the end notes in order to better understand the present subject.

The book, and the entire series, was written as a result of my search for the truth. Having grown up in a major protestant Christian denomination since I was a small child I had been steeped in doctrine which often

times seemed to contradict the very words contained within the Scriptures. I always considered myself to be a Christian although I never took the time to research the origins of Christianity or to understand exactly what the term Christian really meant. I simply grew up believing that Christianity was right and every other religion was wrong or in some way deficient.

Now my beliefs were founded on more than simply blind faith. I had experienced a "living God", my life had been transformed by a loving Redeemer and I had been filled with a powerful Spirit. I knew that I was on the right track, but I always felt something was lacking. I was certain that there was something more to this religion called Christianity; not in terms of a different God, but what composed this belief system which I subscribed to, and this label which I wore like a badge.

Throughout my Christian walk I experienced many highs and some lows, but along the way I never felt like I fully understood what my faith was all about. Sure, I knew that "Jesus died on the cross for my sins" and that I needed to believe in my heart and confess with my mouth in order to "be saved". I "asked Jesus into my heart" when I was a child and sincerely believed in what I had done but again, something always felt like it was missing. As I grew older, I found myself progressing through different denominations, each time learning and growing, always adding some pieces to the puzzle, but never seeing the entire picture.

College ministry brought me into contact with the baptism of the Holy Spirit and more charismatic assemblies yet, while these people seemed to practice a more complete faith than those in my previous denominations, many of my original questions remained unanswered and even more questions arose. It seemed that at each new step in my faith

I added a new adjective to the already ambiguous label "Christian". I went from being a mere Christian to a Full Gospel, New Testament, Charismatic, Spirit Filled, Born Again Christian; although I could never get away from the lingering uneasiness that something was still missing.

For instance, when I read Matthew 7:21-23 I always felt uncomfortable. In that Scripture, the Messiah says: *"Not everyone who says to Me, Lord, Lord, will enter the kingdom of heaven, but he who does the will of My Father Who is in heaven. Many will say to Me on that day, Lord, Lord, have we not prophesied in Your name and driven out demons in Your name and done many mighty works in Your name? And then I will say to them openly (publicly), I never knew you; depart from Me, you who act wickedly [disregarding My commands]."* The Amplified Bible.

This passage of Scripture always bothered me because it sounded an awful lot like the modern day Christian Church, in particular, the charismatic churches which I had been attending where the gifts of the Spirit were operating. According to the Scripture passage it was not the people who *believed* in the spiritual manifestations that were being rejected, it was those who were *actually doing* them. I would think that this would give every Christian pause for concern.

First of all "in that day" there are *many* people who will be calling the Messiah "Lord". They will also be performing incredible spiritual acts in His Name. Ultimately though, the Messiah will openly and publicly tell them to depart from Him. He will tell them that He never knew them and specifically He defines them by their actions, which is the reason for their rejection; they acted wickedly or lawlessly. In short, they disobeyed His commandments. Also, it seems very possible that while

they thought they were doing these things in His Name, they were not, because they may have never known His Name. In essence, they did not know Him and He did not know them.

I think that many Christians are haunted by this Scripture because they do not understand who it applies to or what it means and if they were truly honest they must admit that there is no other group on the face of the planet that it can refer to except for the "Christian Church."

This series provides the answer to that quandary and should provide resolution for any who have suffered anxiety over this verse. Ultimately, my search for answers brought me right back to the starting point of my faith. I was left with the question: "What is the origin and substance of this religion called Christianity?" I was forced to examine the very foundations of my faith and to examine many of the beliefs which I subscribed to and test them against the truth of the Scriptures.

What I found out was nothing short of earth shattering. I experienced a personal parapettio which is a moment in Greek tragedies where the hero realizes that everything he knew was wrong. I discovered that many of the foundations of my faith were not rocks of truth, but rather the sands of lies, deception, corruption and paganism. I saw the Scripture in Jeremiah (Yirmeyahu) come true right before my eyes. In many translations, this passage reads: "*O LORD, my strength and my fortress, My refuge in the day of affliction, The Gentiles shall come to You from the ends of the earth and say, "Surely our fathers have inherited lies, worthlessness and unprofitable things. Will a man make gods for himself, which are not gods?"* Yirmeyahu 16:19-20 NKJV

I discovered that I had inherited lies and false

doctrines from the fathers of my faith. I discovered that the faith which I had been steeped in had made gods which were not gods and I saw very clearly how many could say "Lord, Lord" and not really know the Messiah or do the will of the Father because they rejected His Commandments. I discovered that many of these lies were not just minor discrepancies but critical errors which could possibly have the effect of keeping me out of the New Jerusalem if I continued to practice them. (Revelation 21:27; 22:15).

While part of the problem stemmed from false doctrines which have crept into the Christian religion, it also had to do with anti-Semitism imbedded throughout the centuries and even translation errors in the very Scriptures that I was basing may beliefs upon. A good example is the next verse from the Prophet Jeremiah (Yirmeyahu) where most translations provide: *"Therefore behold, I will this once cause them to know, I will cause them to know My hand and My might; and they shall know that My Name is the LORD."* Yirmeyahu 16:21 NKJV.

Could our Heavenly Father really be telling us that His Name is "The LORD"? This is a title, not a name and by the way, won't many people be crying out "Lord, Lord" and be told that He never knew them? It is obvious that you should know someone's name in order to have a relationship with them. How could you possibly say that you know someone if you do not even know their name. So then we must ask: "What is the Name of our Heavenly Father?" The answer to this seeming mystery lies just beneath the surface of the translated text. In fact, if most people took the time to read the translators notes in the front of their "Bible" they would easily discover the problem.

You see, the Name of our Creator is found in the Scriptures almost 7,000 times, although long ago a false doctrine was perpetrated regarding speaking the Name. It was determined that the Name either could not, or should not, be pronounced and therefore it was replaced. Thus, over the centuries the Name of the Creator which was given to us so that we could know Him and be, not only His children, but also His friends, (Isaiah 41:8, James 2:23, John 15:15) was suppressed and altered. You will now find people using descriptions, titles and variations to replace the Name such as: God, Lord, Adonai, Jehovah and Ha Shem ("The Name") in place of the actual Name which was given in Scriptures. What a tragedy and what a mistake!

One of the Ten Commandments, also known as the Ten Words, specifically instructs us not take the Name of the Creator "in vain" and *"He will not hold him guiltless who takes His name in vain."* (Exodus 20:7). Most Christians have been taught that this simply warns of using the Name lightly or in the context of swearing or in some other disrespectful manner. This certainly is one aspect of the commandment, but if we look further into the Hebrew word for vain - שׁוא (pronounced shav) we find that it has a deeper meaning in the sense of desolating, uselessness or naught.

Therefore, we have been warned not only to avoid using the Name lightly or disrespectfully, but also not to bring it to naught, which is exactly what has been done over the centuries. The Name of our Creator which we have the privilege of calling on and praising has been suppressed to the point where most Believers do not even know the Name, let alone use it.

This sounds like a conspiracy of cosmic proportions and it is. Anyone who believes in the Scriptures must understand that there is a battle between good and evil. There is a Prince of Darkness, Ha Shatan, who understands very well the battle which has been raging since the creation of time. He will do anything to distract or destroy those searching for the truth and he is very good at what he does. He is the Master of Deception and the Father of Lies and he does not want the truth to be revealed. His goal is to steal, kill and destroy. (John 10:10). The enemy has operated openly and behind the scenes over the centuries to infect, deceive, distract and destroy Believers with false doctrine. He truly is a wolf in sheep's clothing and his desire is to rob the Believer of blessings and life.

As you read this book I hope that you will see how he has worked his deception regarding the Sabbath Day. We are given wonderful promises in the Scriptures concerning blessings for those who obey the commandments. Sadly, many Believers have been robbed of those blessings due to false doctrines which teach them to not keep the commandments thus turning them into lawless individuals. Their belief is not followed by righteous works making their faith empty and, to some extent, powerless.

My hope is that every reader has an eye opening experience and is forever changed. I sincerely believe that the truths which are contained in this book and the entire "Walk in the Light Series" are essential to avoid the great deception which is being perpetrated upon those who profess to believe in, and follow the Holy One of Yisra'el.

This book, and the entire series, is intended to be read by anyone who is searching for the truth. Depending upon your particular religion, customs and traditions, you

may find some of the information offensive, difficult to believe or contrary to the doctrines and teachings which you have read or heard throughout your life. This is to be expected and is perfectly understandable but please realize that none of the information is meant to criticize anyone or any faith, but merely to reveal truth.

The information contained in this book had better stir up some things or else there would be no reason to write it in the first place. The ultimate question is whether the contents align with the Scriptures and the will of the Creator. My goal is to strip away the layers of tradition which many of us have inherited and get to the core of the faith which is described in the Scriptures commonly called "The Bible".

This book should challenge your thinking and your beliefs and hopefully aid you on your search for truth. My prayer for you is that of the Apostle Paul (Shaul) in his letter to the Ephesian assembly: *"¹⁷ that the Father of esteem, may give to you the spirit of wisdom and revelation in the knowledge of Him, ¹⁸ the eyes of your understanding being enlightened; that you may know what is the hope of His calling, what are the riches of the glory of His inheritance in the set apart ones,¹⁹ and what is the exceeding greatness of His power toward us who believe, according to the working of His mighty power."* Ephesians 1:17-19.

I

In the Beginning

The subject of the Sabbath is generally misunderstood by those outside of Judaism and as with other topics discussed in the Walk in the Light Series such as Kosher, the "Law" and the Appointed Times, it has historically been treated as something exclusively "Jewish" and inapplicable to Christians. This is due, largely in part, to the man-made doctrine of dispensationalism[1] which creates a bright line distinction between the "Old Testament" and the "New Testament" and attributes things in the "Old Testament" to the "Jews" and things in the "New Testament" to Christians, as if these were two mutually exclusive groups.

This is a false and very divisive doctrine which has sadly permeated much of Christianity. Despite the fact that it has no Scriptural basis it is promoted by many as truth and it changes the way that people read and understand the Scriptures. A person who has been indoctrinated into dispensationalism will be unable to appreciate the simplicity of the Scriptures and the commandments, which become convoluted, twisted, confusing and sometimes incomprehensible when viewed through the lens of this warped theology.

Your own theology may even be influenced by dispensational teaching without you even knowing. It is very subversive and has been used for centuries to explain the division which has existed between "Jews" and Christians since the inception of Christianity. The case of the Sabbath is especially interesting because I do not think that there is any clearer example of a commandment that is so simple to understand and obey, and which was obeyed by early followers of the Messiah. Sadly, the issue of the Sabbath has become so distorted by popular Christian theology that those Christians who actually feel compelled to obey the Fourth Commandment and honor the Sabbath are often spurned as "Sabbath-keepers" or "sabbatarians" and typically classified as heretics or members of a cult.

Through this book it will be revealed that the Sabbath, more accurately called Shabbat (שבת) in Hebrew, is critical to anyone who believes in, and obeys the commandments of the Creator of the Universe (YHWH)[2] as revealed in the Hebrew and Christian Scriptures. Over the centuries, the importance of the Sabbath has been clouded and lost by certain groups due to historical events, doctrines established by organized religion as well as the mistranslation of certain Scripture portions which have been twisted to support the notion that the Sabbath was changed, abolished or strictly applicable to those of "Jewish" descent.

Both Christianity and Judaism claim to serve the same God (Elohim)[3] and both revere the Torah[4] as Scripture, although they do not necessarily use the same names or language.

The Torah, was written by Moses (Mosheh)[5] and consists of the first five (5) books of the Scriptures namely: Genesis (Beresheet), Exodus (Shemot), Leviticus (Vayiqra), Numbers (Bemidbar) and Deuteronomy (Devarim). The Torah is traditionally separated from other Scriptures and is contained in one large scroll although Christianity has combined it into a codex with a collection of writings collectively known as "The Old Testament."[6]

We read in the Torah, that the Sabbath day was blessed and set apart from the beginning of creation. The seventh day of creation was actually the first Shabbat. "[2] *And on the seventh day Elohim completed His work which He had done, and He rested on the seventh day from all His work which He had made.* [3] *And Elohim blessed the seventh day and sanctified it, because on it He rested from His work which Elohim in creating had made.*" Beresheet 2:2-3.

The Hebrew word for sanctified in this verse is qadosh (קדש). It is often translated as "holy," but it more accurately means "to set apart." So the Sabbath is the very first thing that the Scriptures record YHWH setting apart or making holy and the first Sabbath was on the seventh day of creation. Every seventh day from that point onward was a set apart day called the Sabbath.

During the first week of creation Elohim also gave three blessings: He blessed the birds and sea creatures on the fifth day, He blessed Man, both male and female, on the sixth day; and He blessed the seventh Day, the Sabbath. Therefore, not only was the Sabbath set apart, but it was also blessed and the Sabbath existed from the very beginning of creation.

Adam surely knew of the Sabbath, observed the Sabbath and instructed his offspring concerning the

Sabbath. In fact, since man was created on the sixth day then the seventh day was actually the first full day of man's existence. He surely learned from his Creator as they both fellowshipped and rested on the first Shabbat.

2

The Fourth Commandment

The primary commandment concerning Shabbat which most people are familiar with is the Fourth Commandment found within the Ten Commandments.

 The Fourth Commandment is the longest of them all and goes as follows: "*⁸ Remember the Sabbath day, to set it apart. ⁹ Six days you labor and shall do all your work, ¹⁰ but the seventh day is a Sabbath of YHWH your Elohim. You do not do any work - you, nor your son, nor your daughter, nor your male servant, nor your female servant, nor your cattle, nor your stranger who is within your gates. ¹¹ For in six days YHWH made the heavens and the earth, the sea, and all that is in them, and rested the seventh day. Therefore YHWH blessed the Sabbath day and set it apart.*" Shemot 20:8-11. Notice the last sentence which specifically points out that YHWH blessed this day *and* set it apart. In that regard the Sabbath is different from any other day of the weekly cycle.

The Fourth Commandment, along with all of the other commandments were spoken to Yisra'el[7] shortly after the Exodus from Egypt (Mitsrayim)[8] and they were also written down by YHWH and then Mosheh on tablets of stone. Yisra'el consisted of a mixed multitude: descendents from the Twelve Tribes along with foreigners and strangers who had decided to follow YHWH out of Mitsrayim (Shemot 12:28). The Ten Commandments were given to this entire multitude of Yisra'el, because Yisra'el is the redeemed people of YHWH regardless of ethnic origin.

 Accordingly, all were expected to obey, not just the individuals who descended from the Twelve Tribes. This is clearly demonstrated from the passage which states: *"six days do your work, but on the seventh day do not work, so that your ox and your donkey may rest and the slave born in your household, and the alien as well, may be refreshed."* Shemot 23:12 NIV.

This is an important point which must be emphasized: The commandments were given to Yisra'el because they represented the Elect of YHWH. This mixed multitude, which included the physical descendants of Jacob (Ya'akov)[9] along with aliens, strangers and sojourners who joined themselves with the Tribes, was the community of Yisra'el. They were the Redeemed of YHWH who had all been delivered from slavery and given the freedom to obey YHWH in His Kingdom.

If you look at the Scriptures describing how Yisra'el set up camp after the Exodus, you can plainly see that all of the multitude was divided according to the Tribes and there was no separate camp for the aliens and sojourners. Everyone fit within the tribes of Yisra'el and everyone was

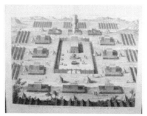 expected to obey the Commandments. Nothing has changed in this regard and if you are one of the Redeemed, whether a physical descendant of Yisra'el or a foreigner who has joined the Kingdom according to the Good News of the Messiah, then you need to obey the commandments including the commandment concerning the Sabbath.[10]

I would think that inclusion within the Ten Commandments would be sufficient enough to compel all Christians to obey and observe the Sabbath, but sadly, this is not the case. Despite the clear and unambiguous language of this commandment, most Christians have been taught to believe that the seventh day Sabbath is "Jewish" and inapplicable to Christians. This notion is simply untrue; the Sabbath has existed since the beginning of time and will continue forever. The fact that the Fourth Commandment begins with "remember" indicates that it existed before Sinai: before the Ten Commandments were given to the mixed multitude that came out of the land of Mitsrayim and we will soon see that it will continue in the future.

3

A Day for All Creation

I was once told by a Rabbi in Jerusalem that a person cannot observe the Sabbath until they convert to the religion of Judaism. His statement was flawed on many levels, but particularly because the Sabbath existed from the beginning of creation, well before there were any "Jews"[11] or even a religion called Judaism. The notion that one must join a man-made religious organization to obey a commandment of YHWH is incorrect. The Sabbath belongs to no man or religion and the Creator wants all of His Creation to observe His Shabbat.

The fact that the Sabbath was intended for all creation is clearly supported by the Scriptures. The Fourth Commandment specifically states: *"In it you shall do no work: you, nor your son, nor your daughter, nor your male servant, nor your female servant, nor your cattle, nor your stranger who is within your gates."* Shemot 20:10. The Sabbath applied to native Yisra'elites as well as to the strangers who sojourned with them, known as ger (גר) in Hebrew. In other words, anyone who intended to dwell with YHWH in His Kingdom needed to observe Shabbat. Notice that if the Sabbath applies to animals, it most certainly would apply to strangers and foreigners who are men and women originally made *"in the image of Elohim."* (Beresheet 1:27).

Read what a popular Christian commentary has to say on this issue. "The mention of a stranger being to observe a Sabbath is a proof that the command of a Sabbath is not merely Jewish, as has frequently been asserted . . . The law of the Sabbath was constituted a memorial of creation: and hence, the reason here assigned must be considered as demonstrating its universal obligation. It is not a reason applicable to any one age, or to one class of men more than to another. All classes of men are bound to obey and glorify the Creator; and the devout observance of the Sabbath is one of the methods divinely appointed for that end."[12]

The prophet Isaiah (Yeshayahu)[13] emphasizes this very important fact when He declares great blessings to: *"the sons of the foreigner who join themselves to YHWH, to serve Him, to be His servants, all who guard the Sabbath, and not profane it, and hold fast to My covenant."* Yeshayahu 56:6. In this text the word used for foreigner is nakar (נכר) which refers to one who was a stranger to the ways of YHWH, often called a heathen or a gentile. Thus, anyone who is a foreigner to YHWH that does not follow His commandments may repent, and turn to Him. When doing so they join with Him which involves guarding the Sabbath and holding fast to His covenant. You hold tight, or bind yourself, to the covenant and you do not let go, even when others tell you that you do not belong or that it does not apply to you.

Yahushua[14], the Hebrew Messiah commonly called Jesus by Christians, confirmed that the Sabbath was for the Gentiles when He cleansed the Temple, also known as the House of YHWH[15]. The following passage is probably one of the most problematic texts in the Messianic Scriptures

for Christians because it seems so inconsistent with the rest of the Gospels. Let us take a look at what happened.

"15 So they came to Jerusalem (Yahrushalayim). Then Yahushua went into the House of YHWH and began to drive out those who bought and sold in the House of YHWH, and overturned the tables of the money changers and the seats of those who sold doves.16 And He would not allow anyone to carry wares through the House of YHWH.17 Then He taught, saying to them, 'Is it not written, My house shall be called a house of prayer for all nations? But you have made it a den of thieves.'" Mark 11:15-17. The Gospel according to John (Yahonatan)[16] describes Yahushua as making a *"whip of cords"* and driving the merchants away. (Yahonatan 2:17).

The question in most people's mind when they read this passage is usually: "What exactly was going on here?" This does not sound like Yahushua, The Suffering Servant (Yeshayahu 53:3) found in the rest of the Gospels. Actually,

 He was giving us a glimpse of The Conquering King Who rules with a rod of iron which we will see more thoroughly during His second coming. (Psalms (Tehillim) 2:9; Revelation 19:11-16). His actions were completely consistent with the dual role that Yahushua the Messiah[17] was meant to fulfill.

He also showed how zealous He was for the House of YHWH. (Psalms (Tehillim) 69:9). To understand the passage you must realize that in that day there was a

custom that people would use the Court of the Gentiles, which was part of the House of YHWH, as a shortcut to carry their goods which were then sold at excessive prices. Many pilgrims traveled a great distance and were unable to physically bring their slaughter offering. They would buy

from the vendors who were in a position to exact high prices from the worshippers. The Scriptures record that all of this was taking place *"in the House of YHWH."* (Yahonatan 2:14). Also, it is speculated by some that the money changers and the merchants were selling to the Gentiles on the Sabbath because it was falsely believed that the Sabbath was not applicable to the Gentiles, who were sometimes referred to as dogs.

In that day, Gentiles were treated as unclean and were restricted in their worship of YHWH. They were not

permitted beyond the Court of the Gentiles under penalty of death as can be read in this Greek inscription which was located at the wall of hostitlity referred to by Shaul (see Ephesians 2:14). In other words, they were not permitted to enter into the House of YHWH as far as the native Yisra'elites which sent a resounding message that they were inferior or not as "special" as a native born Yisra'elite.

Even to this day, the descendents of the Pharisees, the Rabbinic Jews, make no bones about the fact that the Western Wall in Yahrushalayim[18], known as the kotel, is their turf and they can be down right rude to a person who they do not want worshipping in their area. This type of

religious elitism is wrong and not supported by the Torah. It appears that once again, a wall is creating a partition between what some see as a restoration of the Commonwealth of Yisra'el. As a result, many Believers who do not subscribe to Rabbinic Judaism but desire to worship YHWH are finding other places and are surmounting the wall and proceeding to the Mount of the Bais HaMikdash in an effort to get closer to the place where the House of YHWH was once located.

Could it be that we are witnessing the prophecy spoken by Ya'akov over Yoseph: "[22] *Yoseph is a fruitful vine, a fruitful vine near a spring, whose branches climb over a wall.* [23] *With bitterness archers attacked him; they shot at him with hostility.* [24] *But his bow remained steady, his strong arms stayed limber, because of the hand of the Mighty one of Jacob, because of the Shepherd, the Rock of Yisra'el . . .*" Beresheet 49:22-24. Could it be that the Messiah is strengthening Yoseph who has been scattered throughout the world and is now climbing over walls to get to YHWH?

Clearly there was, and remains, a wall between the genetic descendents of the Twelve Tribes of Yisra'el and Gentile Converts. Sadly, this division even exists in some Messianic Congregations which relegate "Gentile

Converts" to associate status while those who can prove their descent from one of the Twelve Tribes may become a full fledged member. Some groups will not even allow a congregation to join unless they have at least 10 members who are "Jewish"[19].

This is sad because it is exactly why the Messiah quoted from the prophet Yeshayahu as He was cleansing the House of YHWH. Let us look at the full text from which He was quoting.

> [1] *Thus says YHWH: 'Keep justice, and do righteousness, for My salvation is about to come, and My righteousness to be revealed.* [2] *Blessed is the man who does this, and the son of man who lays hold on it; who keeps from defiling the Sabbath, and keeps his hand from doing any evil.'* [3] *Do not let the son of the foreigner (Gentile) who has joined himself to YHWH speak, saying, 'YHWH has utterly separated me from His people'; nor let the eunuch say, 'Here I am, a dry tree.'* [4] *For thus says YHWH: 'To the eunuchs who keep My Sabbaths, and choose what pleases Me, and hold fast My covenant,* [5] *Even to them I will give in <u>My house and within My walls</u> a place and a name better than that of sons and daughters; I will give them an everlasting name that shall not be cut off.* [6] *Also the sons of the foreigner (Gentiles) who join themselves to YHWH, to serve Him, and to love the Name of YHWH, to be His servants, all who guard the Sabbath, and not profane it, and hold fast my covenant –* [7] *them I shall bring to My set-apart mountain, and let them rejoice in My house of prayer. Their burnt*

offerings and their slaughterings are accepted on My altar, for My house is called a house of prayer for all people.' Yeshayahu 56:1-7.

In other words, His promises, including the Sabbath, are applicable to all Gentiles *who join themselves to Him* and they are welcome in His House.

This does not mean converting to Judaism, Christianity or any other man-made organized religion. The word translated as "join" in Hebrew is lawah (לוה) which means "to join, to cleave, to abide with, to remain". Therefore you do not join a religion, you "cleave to" YHWH.

By quoting this passage during the cleansing of the House of YHWH, Yahushua is making this point very clear. While many "Jews" observe the Sabbath, it is not a "Jewish" day, it is a set apart day which belongs to YHWH, a day which has been blessed and all creation is welcome to partake in the celebration of the Sabbath.

4

An Appointed Time?

Some believe that the Sabbath is an appointed time based upon the following Scripture. "*And YHWH spoke to Mosheh, saying,* [2] *'Speak to the children of Yisra'el, and say to them: The appointed times of YHWH, which you shall proclaim to be holy convocations, these are My appointed times:* [3] *six days shall work be done, but the seventh day is a Sabbath of solemn rest, a set apart convocation. You shall do no work on it; it is the Sabbath of YHWH in all your dwellings.* [4] *These are the appointed times of YHWH, set apart convocations which you shall proclaim at their appointed times.'*" Vayiqra 23:1-4.

For those unfamiliar with the appointed times, known as moadi (מועדי) in Hebrew, they are set apart gatherings prescribed by YHWH. They are not "Jewish" festivals as is commonly taught. Rather, YHWH calls them His. They belong to Him and calling them "Jewish" is incorrect.

Often the people were called together by silver trumpets (Bemidbar 10:10) to celebrate certain gatherings, particularly times of rejoicing which were called festivals. These gatherings or convocations, included the Feast of Unleavened Bread (Hag Hamatzah - Vayiqra 23:6-8),

Pentecost (Shavuot - Vayiqra 23:15-21), the Day of Trumpets (Yom Teruah – Vayiqra 23:24-25), the Day of Atonement (Yom Kippur - Vayiqra 23:27) and the Feast of Tabernacles (Succot – Vayiqra 23:34-43).[20]

The word "convocation" comes from the Hebrew word miqra (מקרא). It is a set apart assembly or gathering together: it can also mean a rehearsal. Quite often the word convocation appears in the Scriptures, it is preceded by "set apart". Hence, set apart convocation: qadosh miqra (מקרא קדש).

All of these appointed times involve an element of Shabbat and include days which were to be treated as Sabbaths. In other words, you were required to rest on those days just as you would on the Sabbath. The Day of Atonement, called Yom Kippur is one of those days. *"[29] This is to be a lasting ordinance for you: On the tenth day of the seventh month you must deny yourselves and not do any work - whether native-born or an alien living among you - [30] because on this day atonement will be made for you, to cleanse you. Then, before YHWH, you will be clean from all your sins. [31] It is a sabbath of rest, and you must deny yourselves; it is a lasting ordinance. [32] The priest who is anointed and ordained to succeed his father as high priest is to make atonement. He is to put on the sacred linen garments [33] and make atonement for the Most Holy Place, for the Tent of Meeting and the altar, and for the priests and all the people of the community."* Vayiqra 16:29-34. On this day we are instructed to fast as well as rest.

Yom teruah which literally means a day of blowing or shouting. It comes from the word ruwa (רועה) which means to split the ears with sound. *"[23] YHWH said to Mosheh, [24] Say to the Yisra'elites: On the first day of the seventh month you are to have a sabbath, a sacred assembly*

commemorated with trumpet blasts. ²⁵ Do no regular work, but present an offering made to YHWH by fire." Vayiqra 23:23-25. This day is often commemorated by the blowing of a trumpet or a ram's horn, known as a shofar (שופר). It is a rehearsal of the blasts spoken by the Messiah, Shaul and which are prophesied in the Revelation given to Yahonatan.

The first and last day of the feast of Succot are considered Sabbath days. *"³⁹ So beginning with the fifteenth day of the seventh month, after you have gathered the crops of the land, celebrate the festival to YHWH for seven days; the first day is a Sabbath, and the eighth day also is a Sabbath. ⁴⁰ On the first day you are to take choice fruit from the trees, and palm fronds, leafy branches and poplars, and rejoice before YHWH your Elohim for seven days. ⁴¹ Celebrate this as a festival to YHWH for seven days each year. This is to be a lasting ordinance for the generations to come; celebrate it in the seventh month."* Vayiqra 23:39-41.

During the Feast of Unleavened Bread there are two days of rest proscribed by the Scriptures. *"⁵ YHWH's Passover begins at twilight on the fourteenth day of the first month. ⁶ On the fifteenth day of that month YHWH's Feast of Unleavened Bread begins; for seven days you must eat bread made without yeast. ⁷ On the first day hold a set apart assembly and do no regular work. ⁸ For seven days present an offering made to YHWH by fire. And on the seventh day hold a set apart assembly and do no regular work."* Vayiqra 23:5-8.

Shavuot is also a day of rest. *"¹⁵ From the day after the Sabbath, the day you brought the sheaf of the wave offering, count off seven full weeks. ¹⁶ Count off fifty days up to the day after the seventh Sabbath, and then present an offering of new* *grain to YHWH. [17] From wherever you live, bring two loaves made of two-tenths of an ephah of fine flour, baked with yeast, as a wave offering of firstfruits to YHWH. [18] Present with this bread seven male lambs, each a year old and without defect, one young bull and two rams. They will be a burnt offering to YHWH, together with their grain offerings and drink offerings- -an offering made by fire, an aroma pleasing to YHWH. [19] Then sacrifice one male goat for a sin offering and two lambs, each a year old, for a fellowship offering. [20] The priest is to wave the two lambs before YHWH as a wave offering, together with the bread of the firstfruits. They are a sacred offering to YHWH for the priest. [21] On that same day you are to proclaim a sacred assembly and do no regular work." Vayiqra 23:15-21.*

All of these appointed times are quite simply appointments which YHWH has established for those who love and obey Him. While these feasts incorporate elements of the Sabbath within them, it does not necessarily mean that the Sabbath is viewed the same as the feasts.

To emphasize this point, let us take another look at the Scripture cited at the beginning of this chapter. Notice that both Vayiqra 23:2 and 23:4 say virtually the same thing and in essence they "bracket" the middle passage (Vayiqra 23:3) which instructs us to observe the Sabbath on the seventh day. This bracketing is a common Hebrew literary technique called resumptive repetition which, in essence, excludes the Sabbath from the surrounding text that seems to include the Sabbath as one of the moadi. Thus although a simple reading of the text appears to declare the Sabbath as a moadi, a closer look reveals that it is separated and different from the festivals.

This interpretation is consistent with the fact that all of the feasts are harvest oriented celebrations, while the

Sabbath is a weekly convocation. Also, the timing of all of the moadim are contingent upon the lunar cycle and the sighting of the new moon which is very different from the easily determined seventh day Sabbath cycle which has continued since creation. In another text that details the festivals, the Sabbath is not included (Devarim 16) which demonstrates that they are separate and distinct times.

Further, in many other passages, the moadim and the Sabbaths are referred to separately. Some examples are as follows:

- *30 They were also to stand every morning to thank and praise YHWH. They were to do the same in the evening 31 and whenever burnt offerings were presented to YHWH on Sabbaths and at New Moon festivals and at appointed feasts. They were to serve before YHWH regularly in the proper number and in the way prescribed for them. 1 Chronicles (Dibre ha Yamin) 23:30-31.*

- *4 Now I am about to build a House for the Name of YHWH my Elohim and to dedicate it to Him for burning fragrant incense before Him, for setting out the consecrated bread regularly, and for making burnt offerings every morning and evening and on Sabbaths and New Moons and at the appointed feasts of YHWH our Elohim. This is a lasting ordinance for Yisra'el. 2 Chronicles (Dibre ha Yamin) 2:4.*

- *12 On the altar of YHWH that he had built in front of the portico, Solomon sacrificed burnt offerings to YHWH, 13 according to the daily requirement for offerings commanded by Mosheh* for Sabbaths , New Moons and the three annual feasts-the Feast of Unleavened Bread, the Feast of Weeks and the Feast of Tabernacles. 2 Chronicles (Dibre ha Yamin) 8:12-14.

- ² Hezekiyah assigned the priests and Lewites to divisions-each of them according to their duties as priests or Lewites-to offer burnt offerings and fellowship offerings, to minister, to give thanks and to sing praises at the gates of the YHWH's dwelling. ³ The king contributed from his own possessions for the morning and evening burnt offerings and for the burnt offerings on the Sabbaths, New Moons and appointed feasts as written in the Torah of the YHWH. 2 Chronicles (Dibre ha Yamin) 31:2-3.

- ³² We assume the responsibility for carrying out the commands to give a third of a shekel each year for the service of the House of our Elohim: ³³ for the bread set out on the table; for the regular grain offerings and burnt offerings; for the offerings on the Sabbaths, New Moon festivals and appointed feasts; for the holy offerings; for sin offerings to make atonement for Yisra'el; and for all the duties of the house of our Elohim. Nehemiyah 10:32-33.

- ¹³ Stop bringing meaningless offerings! Your incense is detestable to me. New Moons, Sabbaths and convocations - I cannot bear your evil assemblies. ¹⁴ Your New Moon festivals and your appointed feasts my soul hates. They have become a burden to me; I am weary of bearing them. Yeshayahu 1:13-14.

- In any dispute, the priests are to serve as judges

and decide it according to my ordinances. They are to keep my laws and my decrees for all my appointed feasts, and they are to keep my Sabbaths set apart. Yehezqel 44:24.

- *YHWH has made Zion forget her appointed feasts and her Sabbaths.* Lamentations 2:6.

Notice how often the New Moon festival is mentioned along with the Sabbath and the appointed times. The New Moon, otherwise known as Rosh Chodesh (חדש ראש), the head of the month is an important event because it keeps us in tune with the Creator's calendar. Sadly, most of the world lives under a solar calendar system which is oriented around sun god worship. I am pleased to see that people are beginning to rediscover Rosh Chodesh along with the appointed times and the Sabbath.

Thus, while the Sabbath is a very important convocation which permeates all of the moadim, it is not accurate to place it in the same category as one of the festivals. This in no way diminishes the importance of the Sabbath. In fact, due to the frequency and profound significance associated with the Sabbath in the Scriptures, in my opinion, this separation results in its elevation.

5

A Sign

The Sabbath is a sign. *"12 And YHWH spoke to Mosheh, saying, 13 Speak also to the children of Yisra'el, saying: 'Surely My Sabbaths you shall keep, for it is a sign between Me and you throughout your generations, that you may know that I am YHWH who sets you apart. 14 You shall keep the Sabbath, therefore, for it is set apart to you. Everyone who profanes it shall surely be put to death; for whoever does any work on it, that person shall be cut off from among his people.15 Work shall be done for six days, but the seventh is the Sabbath of rest, holy to YHWH. Whoever does any work on the Sabbath day, he shall surely be put to death.16 Therefore the children of Yisra'el shall keep the Sabbath, to observe the Sabbath throughout their generations as a perpetual covenant.17 It is a sign between Me and the children of Yisra'el forever; for in six days YHWH made the heavens and the earth, and on the seventh day He rested and was refreshed.'"* Shemot 31:12-17.

"Moreover I also gave them My Sabbaths, to be a sign between them and Me, that they might know that I am YHWH who sets them apart." Ezekiel (Yehezqel) 20:12. *"Keep my Sabbaths holy (set apart), that they may be a sign between us. Then you will know that I am YHWH your Elohim."* Ezekiel (Yehezqel) 20:20. Notice that the Sabbath is holy, which means set apart, and it is to be kept set apart to YHWH. In other words, it is His day and anyone who follows Him will

observe it as a set apart day. The act of observance makes it a sign or rather a "distinguishing mark" that those who observe the day are set apart to YHWH. In fact, the Hebrew word which is commonly translated "sign" is owt (אות) which means "a mark or a proof."

The word used to describe the Sabbath as a sign is the same word which was used to describe the rainbow (קשתי) as a sign of the covenant made with Noah and all creation. It is also the same word to describe circumcision

 as the sign of the Abrahamic covenant which applies to all of His seed (Galatians 3:29). The owt (אות) of the rainbow and circumcision were meant to be seen and testify of the covenants. Likewise, the Sabbath is meant to be a visible sign of the covenant that YHWH made with His Redeemed.

I can hear the skeptics now protesting that the Sabbath is a sign between YHWH and the children of Yisra'el, not Christians. There is no disputing that fact but the important thing to remember is that when the covenant was established and the commandment was given, there was no such thing as a Christian.

The children of Yisra'el represented the set apart assembly of YHWH on the Earth at that time and the Sabbath was given as a sign between YHWH and the Yisra'elites forever (Shemot 31:17). Semantics are important and it is vital to understand that the Sabbath is not a sign exclusively between YHWH and the adherents of Rabbinic Judaism nor was it made with the modern State of Israel. Rather, the Sabbath is a sign between YHWH and Yisra'el, His Bride which is the Set Apart Assembly of Believers

who love and obey Him.

Many people confuse the Commonwealth of Yisra'el with Rabbinic Judaism or even genetic descendents of one of the Twelve Tribes of Yisra'el, which is a critical mistake. A Yisra'elite is not the same as an adherent to the religion of Judaism nor is a Yisra'elite a person with a certain genetic sequence. A Yisra'elite is a member of the Commonwealth of Yisra'el which is the Kingdom of YHWH often referred to in the Messianic Scriptures as the Kingdom of Heaven or the Kingdom of God.

Besides these semantic issues, the Sabbath existed before there were any people called Hebrews or Yisra'elites. The Sabbath is not subject to any dispensation and transcends any application to a specific grouping based upon genetics, denomination or religion. Rather it is a sign for any and all who believe the promises of the Creator and obey His commandments.

The Sabbath is not currently a sign between YHWH and most Christians which poses a problem because most Christians claim to serve the Elohim of Yisra'el but they do not display the mark of His covenant. Many believe that "The Church" has replaced Yisra'el, but the simple truth is that there are not two classes or groups of Redeemed people, only one. There are not two Brides, only one.

YHWH does not have one plan of redemption for the "Jews" and a different plan of redemption for "the Christian Church". He only has One Body, One Set Apart Assembly, One Yisra'el.[21] There is no question that the Sabbath existed before Sinai and the patriarchs that followed YHWH prior to becoming slaves in Mitsrayim undoubtedly observed the Sabbath. Much of Christianity,

through dispensational influences, has separated from these patriarchs of the faith, mistakenly believing that grace has somehow abolished or changed the relationship that YHWH has with those who serve and obey Him. While He has provided for a perfect atonement through the blood of the Messiah, a method prescribed by the Torah, He still expects His followers to obey Him.

The Messiah did not come to abolish any part of the Torah or the Prophets, rather He came to fill them up with meaning. (Matthew 5:17-20). What was accomplished by His death and resurrection was not an abolition of His Torah but a demonstration of His grace by providing us with the forgiveness and cleansing which we need as the result of our transgression of the Torah. It was the fulfillment of the promise of a renewed covenant with the House of Yisra'el and the House of Yahudah wherein He would put His Torah in their minds and write it on their hearts[22]. He has made provision for us through His covenant and if you want to take hold of the covenant which provides redemption then you had better have the sign of the covenant in your life.

6

An Everlasting Covenant

Aside from the false doctrines of Dispensationalism and Replacement Theology, the Christian religion, save some splinter denominations, is under the mistaken belief that Shabbat was somehow changed from the seventh day of the week (Saturday) to the first day of the week (Sunday). This is in spite of the fact that the Fourth Commandment directs them to keep Shabbat, the seventh day, and there is not one shred of Scriptural authority to indicate that YHWH has rescinded this commandment or altered it in any way. In fact, the Messianic Scriptures and the Tanakh are both filled with passages which confirm that the Sabbath is a perpetual and everlasting commandment.

The Scriptures describe the Sabbath as more than just a sign, it is a covenant. "*[16] The Yisra'elites are to observe the Sabbath, celebrating it for the generations to come as a lasting covenant. [17] It will be a sign between Me and the Yisra'elites forever, for in six days YHWH made the heavens and the earth, and on the seventh day He abstained from work and rested.*'" Shemot 31:16-17. The Hebrew word for covenant is brit (ברית) and the Hebrew word for lasting and perpetual is olaw (עולם) and means: "eternity, forever, without end." The meaning could not be any clearer – The Sabbath is a

covenant which is here to stay.

Again, it was a covenant made with Yisra'el because they were the people who were set apart to YHWH when the command was given. They were also a mixed multitude consisting of many tribes and tongues which all fell under the umbrella of the Twelve Tribes of Yisra'el. The Scriptures do not recount any covenants made with a group of people called Christians. In fact, there are no covenants in any of the Scriptures made with Christians and contrary to popular belief the "New" covenant mediated by the Messiah was not made with Christianity or "The Church" but rather with the House of Yisra'el and the House of Yahudah (Yirmeyahu 31:31-34). There were only Yisra'elites at the Last Supper and the covenant which the Messiah was sealing at that meal was the long awaited renewed or refreshed covenant promised through the Yisra'elite Prophets.

This covenant is integral with the ministry of the Messiah as we shall see later in this discussion. In fact, the Messianic inferences in the passage in Shemot 31:16 are remarkable when you read it in the Hebrew text. Look at how this passage appears in Hebrew:

ושמרו בני ישראל אֵת השבת
לעשות אֵת השבת לדרתם ברית עולם

Notice the two words which are underlined. They are referred to as the Aleph-Taw (אֵת). Aleph (א) is the first letter of the Hebrew alphabet and Taw (ת) is the last letter of the Hebrew alphabet. They are not translated in any of the English versions of the Scriptures. They are not necessarily meant to be translated into any other language

but, in my opinion, are intended to point the reader to the Messiah. This becomes evident when you realize that Yahushua identified himself as the Aleph-Taw in the Book of Revelation on three different occasions (Revelation 1:8, 21:6, 22:13).

Of course, all English translations which came from the Greek manuscripts indicate "Alpha and the Omega" (AΩ) as if the Hebrew Messiah, speaking to His Hebrew Disciple described Himself as a couple of Greek characters. This is a bit unbelievable and it does not have any real Scriptural relevance until you realize that Alpha (A) is the first letter in the Greek alphabet and Omega (Ω) is the last letter in the Hebrew alphabet. Therefore, He was not identifying Himself as the AΩ but rather the את found throughout the Hebrew Scriptures. Armed with this information we see the Messiah embedded within the passage concerning the Sabbath as a perpetual covenant which reinforces the validity and application of the Sabbath to those who believe in the "New" covenant.

Many are confused because they believe that the "New" covenant must have replaced or abolished the "Old" covenant which would, in turn, abolish the Sabbath. This is another example of how semantics can lead to false doctrine. The "New" covenant described in the Messianic Scriptures was a fulfillment of prophesy and a refreshing of the prior covenant made with Yisra'el. Instead of the blood of bulls and goats, YHWH provided the Messiah, a perfect slaughtering, who effected the long awaited atonement for the transgressions of mankind. This fulfillment did not destroy any of the covenants nor the signs of the covenants.

It is a bit absurd to think that YHWH would spend so much time teaching His Elect how to live set apart lives

only to throw it all away and change His instructions. After all, that is what the Torah is, a set of instructions which teach us how to relate to YHWH and with our fellow man. None of this has changed and YHWH has not changed His mind regarding these matters just because Yisra'el transgressed. He does not change (Malachi 3:6), rather He made provision for us through the Messiah and He has given us His Spirit (Ruach) which empowers us to obey.

Yahushua Himself confirmed through His teachings that the Sabbath will remain as a sign for Believers. In the Good News according to Matthew (Mattityahu)[23] Yahushua is quoted as having instructed His followers to: *"Pray that your flight will not take place in winter or on the Sabbath."* Mattityahu 24:20. In this particular passage He was referring to the end of days, a time which has yet to come.

He instructs His followers to pray that their flight does not occur on Shabbat. This must surely mean that Shabbat will still be around during the Tribulation *and* Yahushua will be expecting His followers to be observing Shabbat at that time which will continue to be a sign. A person cannot flee if they are supposed to be resting, that is why we are to pray that our flight will not be on the Sabbath, so that we will not break this commandment.[24]

The Prophet Yehezqel was given a vision of a Bais HaMikdash often called the Third Temple. During the vision he was given instructions regarding the service and the slaughterings. He was informed that the gate of the inner court is to be opened on the Sabbath day and specific offerings are to be made on the Sabbath day (Yehezqel 46). In case you did not realize it, that prophesy has not been fulfilled. It is a future event which we anxiously anticipate.

When it does happen, the Sabbath will be honored and observed.

The Prophet Yeshayahu also speaks of a future time when there is a new heaven and a new earth and we see that time is still reckoned from Sabbath to Sabbath. *"²² As the new heavens and the new earth that I make will endure before me, declares YHWH, so will your name and descendants endure. ²³ From one New Moon to another and from one Sabbath to another, all mankind will come and bow down before me, says YHWH. ²⁴ And they will go out and look upon the dead bodies of those who rebelled against me; their worm will not die, nor will their fire be quenched, and they will be loathsome to all mankind."* Yeshayahu 66:22-24.

This passage is very clear. The Sabbath will continue to the end of time. It was never abolished and those who Believe YHWH should be observing His Sabbath now. It is not hard to observe the commandments and the following chapter will discuss what it means to keep the Sabbath.

7

Keeping the Sabbath

The Sabbath begins after sunset on what we commonly refer to as Friday evening: more accurately called erev (ערב) Shabbat. It continues until the following sunset.[25] Judaism has developed significant traditions surrounding the Sabbath. Most practicing Jews will prepare a nice meal and light two candles prior to the setting of the sun. There are various scripted prayers which are said throughout the evening, on the next morning and at the end of Shabbat. While some of these traditions may be useful and assist the Believer in recognizing the importance of the Sabbath, they are rarely, if ever, commanded by the Scriptures.[26]

In truth, there are very few actual commandments regarding the Sabbath which are found in the Scriptures. We have already read some of the prominent passages including the Fourth Commandment, but here are some others which sum up the essentials: *"¹ Then Mosheh gathered all the congregation of the children of Yisra'el together, and said to them, 'These are the words which YHWH has commanded you to do: ² Work shall be done for six days, but the seventh day shall be a set apart day for you, a Sabbath of rest to YHWH. Whoever does any work on it shall be put to death. ³ You shall kindle no fire throughout your dwellings on the Sabbath day.'"*

Shemot 35:1-3.

The prohibition against work is fairly straightforward. Work would generally include any activity which is intended to make money or which requires physical or mental exertion unrelated to YHWH. There is no master list of prohibited activities and if you try to compile one you are missing the point which is simply: rest and communion with YHWH. Therefore, each person must prayerfully consider their obedience to this commandment.

The prohibition against kindling a fire was directly related to cooking; a task which involved collecting wood, preparing a fire, preparing the food, cooking the food and cleaning up afterward. If women had to prepare meals on the Sabbath then they would not be able to rest. This is why YHWH instructed the children of Yisra'el to gather twice as much manna on the sixth day so they would have enough for the Sabbath, thus avoiding the need to cook.

> [21] *Each morning everyone gathered as much as he needed, and when the sun grew hot, it melted away.* [22] *On the sixth day, they gathered twice as much - two omers for each person - and the leaders of the community came and reported this to Mosheh.* [23] *He said to them, This is what YHWH commanded: Tomorrow is to be a day of rest, a set apart Sabbath to YHWH. So bake what you want to bake and boil what you want to boil. Save whatever is left and keep it until morning.* [24] *So they saved it until morning, as Mosheh commanded, and it did not stink or get maggots in it.* [25] *Eat it today, Mosheh said, because today is a Sabbath to YHWH. You will not find any of it on the ground today.* [26] *six days*

you are to gather it, but on the seventh day, the Sabbath, there will not be any. [27] Nevertheless, some of the people went out on the seventh day to gather it, but they found none. [28] Then YHWH said to Mosheh, How long will you refuse to keep my commands and my instructions? [29] Bear in mind that YHWH has given you the Sabbath; that is why on the sixth day He gives you bread for two days. Everyone is to stay where he is on the seventh day; no one is to go out. [30] So the people rested on the seventh day. Shemot 16:21-30

Using that passage as an example, if you are a child of Elohim you should gather, purchase and cook your food ahead of time so that you can rest on the Sabbath. One of the lessons that we are to learn from observing the Sabbath, and all of the appointed times, is preparation. If we cannot prepare for one day how can we prepare for the Tribulation or eternity for that matter.[27]

The Sabbath is not just a day to abstain from cooking but all labor including our jobs, washing our cars, mowing our lawns and the like. It is a good time to avoid things which are common in order to remember that it is a special day. It is set apart and so we need to treat it as set apart. By doing so, a person is indicating that YHWH is more important than anything else in their lives. At the same time, they are receiving a blessing from their loving Creator. It is a wonderful opportunity for a family to relax and spend quality time together in this fast paced and often chaotic society in which we live.

Buying and selling on the Sabbath is something which is not pleasing to YHWH because it means business

is being transacted when people are supposed to be resting. You can shop on the other six days but the Sabbath is His. An example of this issue is addressed in the Book (Sefer)[28] of Nehemiah (Nehemyah).[29]

> [15] In those days I saw in Judah (Yahudah) those treading wine presses on the Sabbath, and bringing sheaves, and loading donkeys with wine, grapes and figs, and all kinds of burdens, which they brought into Yahrushalayim on the Sabbath day. So I warned them on the day they sold food. [16] And men of Tsor dwelt there, bringing in fish and all kinds of goods, and sold them on the Sabbath to the children of Yahudah, and in Yahrushalayim. [17] Then I contended with the nobles of Yahudah, and said to them, "What evil matter is this that you are doing, profaning the Sabbath Day? [18] Did not your fathers do the same thing so that our Elohim brought all this calamity upon us, and upon this city? Yet you bring more wrath upon Yisra'el by profaning the Sabbath. [19] And it came to pass, that when the gates of Yahrushalayim began to be dark before the Sabbath, I commanded that the gates should be shut, and charged that they should not be opened till after the Sabbath: and some of my servants set I at the gates, that there should no burden be brought in on the Sabbath day. [20] So the merchants and sellers of all kind of ware lodged without Yahrushalayim once or twice. [21] and I warned them and said to them, "Why do you spend the night outside the wall? If you do so again, I will lay hands on you." From that time forth they came no more on the Sabbath. [22] And I

*commanded the Lewites that they should cleanse
themselves, and that they should come and keep
the gates, to sanctify the Sabbath day. Remember
me, O my Elohim, concerning this also, and
pardon me according to the greatness of Your
kindness.* Nehemyah 15:15-22 (original
numbering 13:15-22).

There are a few things going on in that passage.
First, it is clear that the Kingdom of Yahudah was sent into
the Babylonian exile due to the fact that they profaned the
Sabbath. Second, the Children of Yahudah were treading
winepresses and bringing sheaves, wines, grapes and figs
along with other burdens into Yahrushalayim on the
Sabbath. This sounds like it is taking place during the
harvest which would occur around the Feast of Succot.[30]
Even though it is a harvest time, you are still prohibited
from working on the Sabbath. You are also prohibited from
making your animal work. If they are selling their produce
on the Sabbath then they are doing ordinary work on the
Sabbath.

Further, we see men of Tsor, also known as Tyre,
came from Phoenicia which was largely a fishing
community but they were well known as being great
traders. I am sure that they came to Yahrushalayim with
many wonderful products to sell and to them the Sabbath
was no different from any other day. Regrettably, it appears
that their presence in the city was a distraction to the
Yisra'elites and maybe the temptation was too great for
them to ignore. They ended up buying products from the
merchants which not only resulted in the men of Tsor
profaning the Sabbath by working, but the Yisra'elites also
lost sight of the purpose and meaning of the Sabbath.

So it appears then that buying and selling results in profaning YHWH's Sabbath, a day He wants us to remember and keep set apart. Going to restaurants, shopping malls and grocery stores is no way to keep the Sabbath set apart because you are not resting in your dwellings or setting that time apart to YHWH. If you are doing what you want to do, instead of what He wants you to do, on His day you are missing the point and the blessing.

YHWH also commanded rest for the Land of Yisra'el properly referred to as Eretz Yisra'el. *"¹ And YHWH spoke to Mosheh on Mount Sinai, saying, ² Speak to the children of Yisra'el, and say to them: 'When you come into the land which I give you, then the land shall keep a Sabbath to YHWH. ³ Six years you shall sow your field, and six years you shall prune your vineyard, and gather its fruit; ⁴ but in the seventh year there shall be a Sabbath of solemn rest for the land, a Sabbath to YHWH. You shall neither sow your field nor prune your vineyard. ⁵ What grows of its own accord of your harvest you shall not reap, nor gather the grapes of your untended vine, for it is a year of rest for the land. ⁶ And the Sabbath produce of the land shall be food for you: for you, your male and female servants, your hired man, and the stranger who dwells with you, ⁷ for your livestock and the beasts that are in your land - all its produce shall be for food.'"* Vayiqra 25:1-7.

When the children of Yisra'el entered into the promised land, it was supposed to be set apart to YHWH by the observance of a Sabbath. Just as the inhabitants of the nation, including the animals, were to rest every seventh day of each week, so the land which they inhabited was to rest every seven years. Six years they were to sow the field and cut the vineyard, i.e., cultivate the corn-fields, vineyards, and olive-yards (Shemot 23:10) and gather in

their produce; but in the seventh year the land was to keep a Sabbath of rest (Shemot 23:11), a Sabbath consecrated to YHWH, and in this year the land was neither to be tilled nor reaped. It was their failure to give the land its rest which resulted in the exile of Yisra'el from the land (2 Chronicles (Dibre Hayamim) 36:20-21). One way or another, the Word of YHWH will be fulfilled. If we do not obey willingly then YHWH will effect His will. He specifically told the Yisra'elites that if they did not obey then He would scatter them so that the land would enjoy its Sabbath rest (Vayiqra 26:33-35). Yisra'el has experienced this truth many times throughout history and we are all supposed to learn from those mistakes, not repeat them.

Sadly, the Nation of Israel is not currently giving the land a Sabbath rest. Since the inception of the State in 1948 I am not aware of one seven year cycle that the land was given rest. Despite the miraculous creation of a Jewish State, the country is not a Torah observant society. This has many people puzzled as to what role the Modern State of Israel has in the Redemption of Yisra'el. Imagine what a witness and testimony that it would be for them to give the land its Sabbath rest and in turn experience the promised blessings of YHWH. It would mean that in the sixth year the land would produce an enormous bounty large enough to provide for Sabbath year and into the following year until harvest time. This is an often overlooked aspect of Sabbath which has resulted in dire consequences when it was meant to provide incredible blessings.

The rest for the land shows the universal application of the Sabbath. One day when the planet is under the authority and rule of Messiah, I suspect that the whole earth will observe a much needed Sabbath rest and they

will look to the Messiah for His guidance on how to observe the Sabbath. The point of this book is not to tell you how to observe the Sabbath, that would be a mistake. The real purpose of this book is to examine what the Scriptures say about the Sabbath, emphasize the importance of the Sabbath and encourage everyone to observe the Sabbath.

8

Messiah and the Sabbath

The Sabbath is clearly a special day which is demonstrated by the fact that Yahushua was resurrected on a Sabbath, not Easter Sunday which is and always has been a day for pagan celebrations.[31] Yahushua also spent a great deal of time prior to His resurrection and ascension teaching on the subject of the Sabbath. Because this is such an important issue to the Father, Yahushua spent much time distinguishing between the traditions of men and proper observance of the Sabbath. He never taught that we should not obey the Sabbath, nor did He ever indicate that He was going to change the Sabbath. In fact, He always observed the Sabbath, just not the way the Pharisees thought He should.

In order to understand the teachings of Yahushua on this subject, it is important to remember the purpose of the Sabbath. It is a set apart day, a day of rest and refreshing primarily: both physically and spiritually. This does not specifically mean that the Sabbath is the day to congregate outside of your home as Catholics and Christians treat Sunday. Traditionally, Yisra'elites who lived in Yahrushalayim would go to the House of YHWH while those outside Yahrushalayim would gather together in what has commonly been called a "Synagogue."[32]

The act of assembling is certainly appropriate, although there is nothing wrong with a family remaining home, resting, congregating, worshipping and studying without going anywhere. When it takes hours to get you and your family ready and then travel back and forth from assembling, you can probably forget about getting much rest. It is not absolutely essential that you assemble on this day if it means that you will not be able to rest. The main thing is to make certain that you get rest and that your focus is on YHWH.

There is nothing wrong with congregating on any day, so long as you properly observe the Sabbath on the correct day, the seventh day. The Messiah always observed the Sabbath and, *"as His custom was, He went into the congregation on the Sabbath day, and stood up to read."* Luke 4:16. He healed on the Sabbath (Luke 13:14), He taught on the Sabbath (Mark 1:21) and He gave instruction on how to properly observe the Sabbath. (Mattityahu 12; Luke 6).

He often got into disputes with the Pharisees concerning this issue because this is an especially important subject for the Messiah. For further insight let us look at some additional Scriptures which detail Yahushua and His treatment of the Sabbath. *"¹ Now it happened on the second Sabbath after the first that He went through the grain fields. And His disciples plucked the heads of grain and ate them, rubbing them in their hands. ² And some of the Pharisees said to them, 'Why are you doing what is not lawful to do on the Sabbath?' ³But Yahushua answering them said, 'Have you not even read this, what David (Dawid) did when he was hungry, he and those who were with him: ⁴ how he went into the house of YHWH, took and ate the showbread, and also gave some to those with him, which is not lawful for any but the priests to eat?'*

⁵ And He said to them, 'The Son of Adam (Man) is also Master (Lord) of the Sabbath.'" Luke 6:1-5.

The Disciples were not violating the Torah by plucking grain to eat but their actions were prohibited according to the Pharisaic tradition. The Pharisees were so caught up in their own man-made traditions, customs and interpretations that they became more concerned with their own rules than with the Torah. We now see this same error being perpetuated throughout Rabbinic Judaism and this was the underlying point in most of the disputes between Yahushua and the Pharisees.

Another interesting part of this passage is when Yahushua refers to Himself as "Master of the Sabbath" which some translations interpret as "Lord of the Sabbath"[33]. It is important to determine what He means by "Master of the Sabbath" because for some reason I have heard numerous Christians quote this Scripture to support the notion that the Sabbath was changed to Sunday. On the surface, I see nothing that would lend support to that argument. The only connection that I can see is that Christians who incorrectly believe that Yahushua was resurrected on Sun Day or "The Lord's Day" believe that the title of "Lord of the Sabbath" or "Master of the Sabbath" must somehow mean that the "new" Christian Sabbath is Sunday. This is extremely convoluted and faulty logic and is not supported by the text.

By claiming to be "Master of the Sabbath" Yahushua is actually acknowledging and confirming the perpetual relevance of the Sabbath. If the Sabbath were unimportant or abolished then He would have been declaring Himself "Master of Nothing." This was obviously not His intent, rather Yahushua was declaring

that He is the One who determines what is proper and improper to do on the Sabbath. By calling Himself "Master of the Sabbath", He is proclaiming His authority because this day belongs to YHWH. If He has the power to control the Sabbath then He is Sovereign. Therefore, Yahushua being called "Master of the Sabbath" has nothing to do with the establishment of Sunday worship and everything to do with the fact that He is King.

Most scholars of faith will agree that the Earth is approximately 6,000 years old. Believers anticipate the Messiah coming soon and when He does, He will establish His reign *"on Earth as it is in Heaven."* (Luke 11:2). This is known as the millennial reign or the millennial kingdom and will be the Sabbath millennium. The Apostle Peter (Kepha)[34] stated: *"With YHWH a day is like a thousand years, and a thousand years are like a day."* 2 Kepha 3:8. This is another reason why Yahushua is Master of the Sabbath. He was born during the Sabbath month[35], He was resurrected on the Sabbath day, He will return during the Sabbath month[36] and He will reign over the Sabbath millennium.[37]

The teachings of Yahushua regarding the Sabbath were meant to demonstrate the real purpose of the Sabbath and to tear down the impediments which were attached to this particular commandment by men. As we see through the ministry of Yahushua, men, and particularly the religious leaders of the day, were good at appearances. To show how pious they were they would often add to the Torah.

In an effort not to violate any of the commandments, they "built a fence" around the Torah, which means that they developed a new set of regulations

intended to keep people far away from violating any of the commandments. While this may seem like a noble endeavor, it is really quite presumptuous and a clear violation of the Torah when it involves adding to the Torah, which is often exactly what happens. As a result, men start learning, studying and obeying the man-made regulations which then diminish and supersede the clear instructions found within the Torah itself.

By the time that Yahushua walked the earth in the flesh, men had established hundreds of rules concerning the Sabbath while the Torah only provided a few. The Sabbath is a prime example of how the religious leaders placed heavy burdens on the children of Yisra'el and replaced the freedom of simple obedience with man made rules which led to bondage. Today, Rabbinic Judaism has over 1,500 regulations surrounding the Sabbath. What was originally intended as a protective fence has become a seemingly insurmountable barrier.

This is what Yahushua stated concerning this practice. "[46] *Woe to you also, you lawyers (experts in the law)! For you load men with burdens hard to bear, and you yourselves do not touch the burdens with one of your fingers. [47] Woe to you! For you build the tombs of the prophets, and your fathers killed them. [48] In fact, you bear witness that you approve the deeds of your fathers; for they indeed killed them, and you build their tombs. [49] Therefore the wisdom of Elohim also said, 'I will send them prophets and apostles, and some of them they will kill and persecute,' [50] that the blood of all the prophets which was shed from the foundation of the world may be required of this generation, [51] from the blood of Abel to the blood of Zekaryah who perished between the altar and the temple. Yes, I say to you, it shall be required of this generation. [52] Woe to you lawyers (experts in the law)! For you have taken away the key of*

knowledge. You did not enter in yourselves, and those who were entering in you hindered." Luke 11:46-52.

A prophet generally came to warn and direct people back to YHWH. They often pointed the error of people's ways which usually were rooted in the leadership. If people repented YHWH would usually restore them although His perfect justice required punishment. Often times, the leaders who had established themselves through deception and falsehood, relied upon those lies to preserve and maintain their power. Repentance would mean a restoration of truth and a loss of position, prestige, wealth etc. Many times they would simply kill the prophet in an attempt to shut them up. They did not want to change; they liked things exactly as they were.

Therefore, Yahushua was stating that the religious leaders and their fathers had been warned. Their fathers killed the prophets and the present day leaders were reaffirming those actions by building their tombs. Neither had a desire to know the truth. Instead of following the Torah, which was equally applied to men, they preferred to create and enforce their own rules which empowered them and allowed them to wield authority over others. Instead of leading people to YHWH they were crushing them with their traditions which resulted in a perversion of the truth.

A clear example of this conflict between the commandments of men and the commandments of YHWH can be seen when Yahushua healed the invalid on the Sabbath. *"⁸ Then Yahushua said to him, 'Get up! Pick up your mat and walk.' ⁹ At once the man was cured; he picked up his mat and walked. The day on which this took place was a Sabbath, ¹⁰ and so the Yahudim said to the man who had been healed, 'It is the Sabbath; the law forbids you to carry your*

mat.' ¹¹ But he replied, 'The man who made me well said to me, Pick up your mat and walk.'" Yahonatan 5:8-11. Yahushua healed a man and specifically told him to pick up his mat and walk. The Torah does not prohibit a person from picking up their mat and walking, especially when they have just been miraculously healed by the Messiah. It was only the tradition of men which could possibly forbid such a thing.

It had gotten so bad that the Scribes and Pharisees even argued that it was unlawful to heal on the Sabbath. "⁶ Now it happened on another Sabbath, also, that He entered the synagogue and taught. And a man was there whose right hand was withered. ⁷ So the Scribes and Pharisees watched Him closely, whether He would heal on the Sabbath, that they might find an accusation against Him. ⁸ But He knew their thoughts, and said to the man who had the withered hand, 'Arise and stand here.' And he arose and stood. ⁹ Then Yahushua said to them, 'I will ask you one thing: Is it lawful on the Sabbath to do good or to do evil, to save life or to destroy?' ¹⁰ And when He had looked around at them all, He said to the man, 'Stretch out your hand.' And he did so, and his hand was restored as whole as the other. ¹¹ But they were filled with rage, and discussed with one another what they might do to Yahushua." Luke 6:6-11.

Imagine that! The religious leaders were so blinded by their own unhealthy legalistic mindset that they failed to recognize or appreciate the miracles which were occurring before their eyes. Instead, they were condemning the Messiah for healing on this special day. Yahushua surely must have been grieved when He was confronted by such attitudes, especially because these were the ones teaching His people. The Sabbath which YHWH created for good was meant to be an easy commandment for His people to bear (Mattityahu 11:30). Sadly, it had been turned

 45

into a heavy weight around men's necks by the religious leaders (Acts 15:10). The Sabbath was meant to give needed rest and refreshing to YHWH's creation and what better time to heal His people than on this blessed, set apart day.

It seems utterly ridiculous that anyone would ever believe that YHWH would prohibit healing on the Sabbath. The reason that this is so bizarre is that all true healing comes from YHWH, so if a person gets healed on the Sabbath, then it surely has come from YHWH. This just goes to show how far Yisra'el had strayed from the truth by the time Yahushua came in the flesh.

It must have angered Him to see how men had twisted His commands which were meant to liberate and bless His people. Instead of providing rest, the traditions of men were enslaving His people. This is exactly what He was referring to when He said: "*28 Come to Me, all you who labor and are heavy laden, and I will give you rest. 29 Take My yoke upon you and learn from Me, for I am gentle and lowly in heart, and you will find rest for your souls. 30 For My yoke is easy and My burden is light.*" Mattityahu 11:28-30 NKJV.

This rest that He was promising was the rest that was to be found through Shabbat. As Master of the Sabbath He was telling people to throw off the yoke which men had placed upon them through their ordinances and traditions and let Him guide and instruct them through His Torah to true Sabbath observance. He made this statement on a Sabbath and immediately prior to His most significant teachings on the Sabbath. (Mattityahu 12:1-13; Luke 6:1-10).

Often times we do not know what is best for us, but our Creator does. This call to rest is meant to be a blessing. He created this extraordinary day for our benefit. He blessed this day and it was meant to be a blessing to us.

This is what Yahushua meant when He said *"The Sabbath was made for man, not man for the Sabbath"* Mark 2:27. In fact, Yahushua taught that it was lawful to do good on the Sabbath. *"¹¹ If any of you has a sheep and it falls into a pit on the Sabbath, will you not take hold of it and lift it out? ¹² How much more valuable is a man than a sheep! Therefore it is lawful to do good on the Sabbath."* Mattityahu 12:11-12.

In every way the Messiah affirmed the truth and importance of the Sabbath. He asserted His authority over the Sabbath by expressing the fact that He is Master of the Sabbath. If the Messiah is your Master then it would only make sense that you would keep the Sabbath as He instructed.

9

Early Believers and the Sabbath

Yahushua always revered the Torah and He always observed the Sabbath. If there is anyone in history who understood the teachings of Yahushua as they related to the Sabbath I would suppose that it would be the original disciples who followed Yahushua and heard His teachings. Those disciples continued to observe the Sabbath after His death and resurrection.

Early followers of Yahushua were all Yisra'elites for many years. They were a sect of Yisra'el often called Nazarenes, Natsarim or simply followers of "The Way". They observed the Torah and specifically they observed the Sabbath. This is sometimes hard to discern because of certain unscriptural doctrines which have pervaded the Christian religion for centuries. The following are some clear examples from the Messianic Scriptures concerning the Sabbath observance of the original Believers.

"Then they went home and prepared spices and perfumes. But *they rested on the Sabbath in obedience to the commandment.*" Luke 23:56 NIV.

"After the Sabbath, at dawn on the first day of the week, Mary Magdalene and the other Mary went to look at the tomb" Mattityahu 28:1 NIV. They waited to go to the tomb because they were resting, in observance of the

Sabbath. Since the Sabbath ended at sundown and there were no streetlights, it would only make sense that two women would wait until sunrise to travel. These were followers of Yahushua who heard His teachings and observed His ways. If they were observing the Sabbath even after His death, when they desperately wanted to get to the tomb, then clearly they understood that the Sabbath was a continuing mandate.

An erroneous interpretation of the following passage in the Book of Acts is often used to support the belief that the Sabbath was changed to Sunday. "*⁷ Now on the first day of the week, when the disciples came together to break bread, Shaul, ready to depart the next day, spoke to them and continued his message until midnight.⁸ There were many lamps in the upper room where they were gathered together.*" Acts 20:7-8. This verse is construed by some to support the move from the Sabbath (seventh day) to the Lord's Day (first day) since the Disciples "broke bread" on the first day of the week.

In order to properly understand this passage you need to understand the correct reckoning of time as well as Hebraic tradition. While the modern system considers midnight to be the beginning of a new day, the Scriptural day begins after sunset, typically when three stars are visible in the sky. Thus, the new day actually begins in the evening.

Traditionally, when the Sabbath ends at the setting of the sun on the seventh day (Saturday) many people continue to fellowship with a meal (ie. break bread), because it is then permissible to cook. Although the setting of the sun signifies the beginning of first day of the week and work can be done, most people do not go to work

because it is dark. As a result, many people continue to fellowship and break bread after the Sabbath. The time after the Sabbath when the sun is set is called havdallah, which means "separation".

Some people observe a special ceremony to commemorate the passing of the Sabbath which is then followed by fellowship and a meal. This meal, according to Jewish tradition, is called the Melaveh Malka and it means "accompanying the queen." "Partaking in this meal is an additional way of bidding farewell to the Sabbath. According to legend, the custom originated with King David. David asked God when he would die, and God told him it would be on a Sabbath. From that time on, when each Sabbath was over, David made a party to celebrate his survival. The nation at large rejoiced with him and adopted the practice of celebrating the Melaveh Malka on Saturday night."[38]

This is generally what the disciples were doing in the passage in Acts. After the Sabbath was over and it was dark, they remained together for fellowship and a meal. Shaul would be leaving the next morning at first light to continue his travels so he spent his last waking hours, which was the first day of the week, sharing and teaching until midnight. In this particular passage a great miracle occurred when Eutychus was raised from the dead after falling out of a third story window. Understandably, nobody went to bed and they all talked until daylight (Acts 20:9-12).

It is generally accepted that the Book of Acts was written by Luke in about 70 to 80 A.D., well after the death and resurrection of Yahushua. In the first Chapter of Acts, Luke recounts the ascension of Yahushua and states: [12]

Then they returned to Yahrushalayim from the hill called the *Mount of Olives, a Sabbath day's walk from the city."* Acts 1:12. Now the ascension did not occur on a Sabbath so there was no particular reason to make mention of the distance except to reaffirm that they were still observing the Sabbath and still gauged distance by how far it was permitted to walk on the Sabbath which, by the way is more a matter of accepted tradition than an actual commandment.

Gentile converts were no different than the native Yisra'elites. They were expected to go to Synagogue on the Sabbath and learn the Torah along with the Hebrew Believers. *"[19] Therefore I judge that we should not trouble those from among the Gentiles who are turning to Elohim, [20] but that we write to them to abstain from things polluted by idols, from sexual immorality, from things strangled, and from blood. [21] For Mosheh (the Torah) has had throughout many generations those who preach him in every city, being read in the congregations every Sabbath."* Acts 15:19-21.[39]

All of these Scriptures support the fact that followers of Messiah Yahushua observed the seventh day Sabbath, whether they were native born Yisra'elites or Gentile converts. Some theologians have tried to explain this glaring contradiction in Christian history by creating an Apostolic Dispensation. They teach that there was a dispensation (period of time) when the apostles continued to obey the Torah until the Temple was destroyed in 70 A.D.

While on the surface this may sound like a rational explanation for the Christian doctrinal inconsistency, it is absolutely wrong. Instead of simply admitting that modern Christianity is in error and restoring the truth concerning

the Sabbath, theologians have created new doctrines and interpretations to patch up and prop up the false teachings inherited from their predecessors. This has been going on for centuries and I hear the cry of the prophet Jeremiah (Yirmeyahu)[40] as he declares: *"The Gentiles shall come to You from the ends of the earth and say, 'Surely our fathers have inherited lies, worthlessness and unprofitable things.'"* Yirmeyahu 16:19 NKJV. As you will read in the upcoming chapters, Christians truly have inherited lies concerning the Sabbath.

IO

Paul and the Sabbath

Christianity often looks to the writings of Paul (Shaul)[41] to justify their dispensational beliefs which lead to their rejection of the Torah. Sadly, the writings of Shaul are often mistranslated or twisted in order to support these false doctrines. The reason being that his letters are often complicated and difficult to understand, particularly if they are not viewed in the proper cultural and Scriptural context. In my opinion, they cannot be understood unless a person has a solid understanding of the Tanakh.

Even Kepha proclaimed: *"[15] . . . our beloved brother Shaul, according to the wisdom given to him, has written to you,[16] as also in all his epistles, speaking in them of these things, in which are some things hard to understand, which untaught and unstable people twist to their own destruction, as they do also the rest of the Scriptures."* 2 Kepha 3:14-16. Thus, even while the Disciples were still alive people were twisting the words of Shaul. Imagine how far it has come in the past 1,900 years.

Let us begin with a fundamental passage that Shaul wrote in the Epistle to the Hebrews regarding the Sabbath and see how it has been mistranslated to the point where it does not even say what was intended. The New King James Translation reads as follows: *"There remains therefore a rest*

for the people of God." Hebrews 4:9 NKJV. This passage does not really mean very much to most readers and is often used in support of the notion that Sunday is now the Sabbath or that every day is a Sabbath. We will get to these arguments a bit further on in the discussion, but for now I want to look a little deeper into the translation of the passage in his letter to the Hebrews (Ibrim - עברים).

An accurate interpretation of the Greek text reads as follows: *"So there remains a Sabbath-keeping for the people of Elohim."* (The Scriptures).[42] The word sabbatismos (σαββατισμός) appears in the Greek from a derivative of sabbaton (σαββατον) which is from the Hebrew word shabbat. Shabbat means Sabbath, it does not mean rest. While rest is one of the things intended to occur on the

 Sabbath, the meanings are not interchangeable. The Sabbath always was and remains the seventh day of the week, currently known as Saturday, or Saturn's Day on the Roman pagan calendar. The Romans dedicated this day to one of their deities and the modern world has continued that pagan custom.

The word for rest in the Greek is katapausis (καταπαυσισ) which is used in many of the surrounding portions in Hebrews (Ibrim) and in those cases it is properly translated as "rest". In Ibrim 4:9 though, the Greek word is not katapausis (καταπαυσισ), but rather sabbatismos (σαββατισμός). Most modern English translations have taken out the word Shabbat, which has a very important and specific meaning, and replaced it with the very vague and general term "rest."

The exclusion of the word Shabbat from most translations is a critical error. Let us now look at the entire quote from Shaul, in context, to see if we can determine the message that he is trying to convey.

¹ Therefore, since a promise remains of entering into His rest, let us fear lest any of you seem to have come short of it.² For indeed the Good News was brought to us as well as to them; but the word which they heard did not profit them, not having been mixed with belief in those who heard it. ³ For we who have believed do enter into that rest, as He has said: 'As I swore in My wrath, if they shall enter My rest . . .' And yet His works have come into being from the foundation of the world.⁴ For somewhere He has said thus about the seventh day, 'And Elohim rested on the seventh day from all His works,' ⁵ and in this again, 'If they shall enter into My rest . . .' ⁶ Since then it remains for some to enter into it, and those who formerly received the Good News did not enter in because of disobedience, ⁷ He again defines a certain day, 'Today', saying through Dawid (David) so much later, as it has been said, 'Today if you hear His voice, do not harden your hearts.' ⁸ For if Yahushua had given them rest, He would not have spoken of another day after that. ⁹ So there remains a Sabbath-keeping for the people of Elohim. ¹⁰ For the one, having entered into His rest, has himself also rested from his works, as Elohim rested from His own.¹¹ Let us therefore do our utmost to enter into that rest, lest anyone fall after the same example of disobedience. Ibrim 4:1-11

The text is clear, we are to enter into the Sabbath rest just as Elohim rested. Believers are to be obedient to the commandment in contrast to those who did not enter in because of disobedience. Shaul is reinforcing the commandments concerning the Sabbath and is not teaching anything contrary to the Torah. Notice also that he emphasizes the Creation week which emphasizes the point that the Sabbath began at creation, not at Sinai.

An Epistle of Shaul which is often used to support the notion of Sunday worship is found in the First Letter to the Corinthians. *"¹ Now concerning the collection for the set apart ones (saints), as I have given orders to the assemblies of Galatia, so you must do also: ² On the first day of the week let each one of you lay something aside, storing up as he may prosper, that there be no collections when I come."* 1 Corinthians 16:1-3.

Again, it is important to recognize that the Scriptural day starts at sundown. The Sabbath begins at sundown after the sixth day (Friday evening) and ends at sundown the following day (Saturday evening). You are not supposed to conduct business during the Sabbath and some Yisra'elites would not even carry money on the Sabbath. Therefore, it would be natural that any business would be conducted on the first day of the week, immediately after Sabbath (Saturday evening), while the Believers were still together.

This was purely an administrative matter which made good sense. Since the Believers would be fellowshipping during the Sabbath, they would not abruptly end their fellowship at sundown when the first day of the week began. It was dark, and no real work could be done so they would typically continue their fellowship and also the elders could deal with the business aspects of

the Assembly. It was a natural occurrence and certainly did not mean that the Sabbath had changed to Sunday. In fact, this passage supports the fact that the Believers were still observing the Sabbath because they were not handling money on the Sabbath, they were waiting until Sabbath was over and the first day of the week began in order to take care of their finances.

Another writing which is often used to justify Sunday worship, or the abolition of the seventh day Sabbath, is found in Romans 14. "*¹ Accept him whose faith is weak, without passing judgment on disputable matters. ² one man's faith allows him to eat everything, but another man, whose faith is weak, eats only vegetables. ³ The man who eats everything must not look down on him who does not, and the man who does not eat everything must not condemn the man who does, for Elohim has accepted him. ⁴ Who are you to judge someone else's servant? To his own master he stands or falls. And he will stand, for the Lord is able to make him stand. ⁵ one man considers one day more sacred than another; another man considers every day alike. Each one should be fully convinced in his own mind. ⁶ He who regards one day as special, does so to YHWH. He who eats meat, eats to YHWH, for he gives thanks to Elohim; and he who abstains, does so to YHWH and gives thanks to Elohim.*" Romans 14:1-6. This passage is more difficult than the others if you do not understand the context in which it was written.

"The reference is not specifically to Jewish holidays but to any days that any believer might have come to regard as especially holy. This is because the 'weak' are not specifically Jewish believers, but any believers attached to particular calendar observances."[43] "*Days include fast days enjoined in the Torah and/or by the Sages (cf Ta'anit) or other minor remembrances (cf. Judges 11:40); days*

considered to be under lucky, or unlucky stars according to the astrological calendar; or to the pagan holidays dedicated to the numerous gods within the Roman pantheon . . . Certain (Jewish and Gentile) Hellenistic circles practiced a religiously-based vegetarianism combined with abstinence from wine, and a belief in astrology connected with a fear of demons which made some days lucky and other days unlucky. Paul's argument here is influenced on the one hand by Hellenistic Jewish ideas such as Philo's, and a debate between the two Pharisaic schools of Beit Shammai and Beit Hillel. Philo associates religious dietary habits with the observance of holy days . . ."[44]

You have to read more than just one verse for this passage to make sense. Once you read the entire portion and gather enough information to see the proper backdrop it becomes plain that Shaul was dealing with some very specific issues that had arisen within the Assembly in Rome, a society which was surrounded with pagan practices and beliefs. He was addressing an issue regarding observances and practices which fell outside of the Torah and derived from the Roman culture, not the Sabbath which is clearly proscribed by the Scriptures. He prefaced the discussion by referring to the issues as "disputable matters". The Sabbath is clearly not a disputable matter, it was literally "etched in stone".

A similarly mistranslated text is found in Shaul's letter to the Galatians: "*You observe days and months and seasons and years.*" Galatians 4:10. Many interpret this passage to read as if Shaul were chastising the Galatians for observing the Sabbath. Once again, you must read the Scripture in context and in its entirety as follows: "[8] *But then, indeed, when you did not know Elohim, you served those*

which by nature are not gods.⁹ But now after you have known Elohim, or rather are known by Elohim, how is it that you turn again to the weak and beggarly elements, to which you desire again to be in bondage? ¹⁰ You observe days and months and seasons and years.¹¹ I am afraid for you, lest I have labored for you in vain." Galatians 4:8-11.

Shaul is writing to Gentile pagan converts, not Hebrew Believers. It is clear that the "weak and beggarly elements" that Shaul is referring to are the pagan days, months, seasons and years relating to the false gods that they once served. This passage has nothing to do with the Sabbath.

One passage which specifically refers to the Sabbath but is subject to poor translation is found in the Letter to the Colossians. In this instance the poor translation is responsible for changing the meaning of the passage. First we will look at a popular translation and then we will examine the literal translation from the Greek Text. *"¹⁶ So let no one judge you in food or in drink, or regarding a festival or a new moon or sabbaths, ¹⁷ which are a shadow of things to come, but the <u>substance</u> (is) of Christ."* Colossians 2:16-17 NKJV.

This passage appears to say that we are not to judge others on their "Christian liberty". The implication is that the festivals (appointed times), the new moon and the Sabbath are not important anymore, because they are only shadows and the real substance is Christ (Messiah). That is an erroneous interpretation. The word substance is not a correct translation for the Greek word "soma" (soma) which means "body". Also, the word "is" is not found in the original text and was added by translators to make the passage mean what they wanted it to mean.

The literal interpretation of the passage from the

Greek reads as follows: "*¹⁶ Then do not let anyone judge you in eating, or in drinking, or in part of a feast, or the new moon, or of Sabbaths, ¹⁷ which is a shadow of things coming, but the body of Messiah.*" Now the meaning is crystal clear. Since all of these matters are a shadow of things to come and are all spiritual in nature, do not let anyone outside the Body of Messiah judge in these matters, because only the Body of Messiah is in a position to properly understand and judge concerning those things.

At the time this letter was written, the Believers in Colossae were living in the midst of a pagan sun god worshipping society. When they began observing the Torah, they set themselves apart from the rest of their society by observing Scriptural commandments and abstaining from pagan practices. So then, this statement from Shaul is meant to encourage them in their Torah observance, not discourage them. He is telling them not to be concerned about the judgments coming from the pagans around them because their Scriptural observances were spiritual shadows only understood by members of the Body of Messiah. He also may be warning them against Judaizers who were constantly trying to ensnare Believers into obeying the man made commandments and traditions which would put them under the law and bondage.

Therefore, all the writings of Shaul, when accurately translated and viewed in their proper context, support the continuation of the Sabbath and in no way indicate that Believers should not be observing the Sabbath.

Contrary to popular belief, Shaul never taught against the Torah or the Sabbath. In fact, he was a Torah observant Hebrew who always observed the Sabbath. Let us examine some Scripture passages which support this

assertion.

- *¹³ Now when Shaul and his party set sail from Paphos, they came to Perga in Pamphylia; and Yahonatan, departing from them, returned to Yahrushalayim. ¹⁴ But when they departed from Perga, they came to Antioch in Pisidia, and went into the synagogue on the Sabbath day and sat down. Acts 13:13-14.*

- *⁴² As Shaul and Barnabas (Barnabah) were leaving the synagogue, the people invited them to speak further about these things on the next Sabbath. ⁴³ When the congregation was dismissed, many of the Yahudim and devout converted worshippers followed Shaul and Barnabas (Barnabah), who talked with them and urged them to continue in the grace of Elohim. ⁴⁴ On the next Sabbath almost the whole city gathered to hear the word of YHWH. Acts 13:42-44.*

- *On the Sabbath we went outside the city gate to the river, where we expected to find a place of prayer. Acts 16:13.*

- *As his custom was, Shaul went into the synagogue, and on three Sabbath days he reasoned with them from the Scriptures. Acts 17:2.*

- *Every Sabbath he reasoned in the congregation, trying to persuade Yahudim and Greeks. Acts 18:4.*

These Scriptures acknowledge that the seventh day was still considered to be the Sabbath when Shaul was ministering and when the Book of Acts was written. He also made every effort to go to Yahrushalayim to observe the appointed times as can be seen throughout the Book of Acts. He did not continue to observe the Sabbath because

he was in some special advent carved out for the Early Hebrew Apostles. He kept the Sabbath because he was a follower of the Messiah who was The Master of the Sabbath.

II

Sunday – The Lord's Day

With all of the evidence provided thus far the question must be asked: Why doesn't Christianity properly observe the Sabbath? The answer is actually quite simple and well documented. After centuries of organized religion had a chance to settle in, men eventually attempted to change this command which, of course, is not possible. Whether men choose to observe the Sabbath or not is of no consequence: the Sabbath is still the Sabbath. Make no mistake about the fact that the Catholic and Christian practice of worshipping on Sunday, the day customarily attributed to sun god worship, is simply a tradition created by men. It was man that attempted to replace the Sabbath with Sunday, not Yahushua or Shaul.

"Traditionally the adoption of Sunday observance in place of the seventh-day Sabbath has been attributed to ecclesiastical authority rather than to Biblical precept or mandate. Thomas Aquinas (d. 1274), for example, states categorically: 'In the New Law the observance of the Lord's day took the place of the observance of the

Sabbath, not by virtue of the precept [Fourth Commandment] but by the institution of the Church.' The same view was reiterated three centuries later in the Catechism of the Council of Trent (1566) which states, 'It pleased the Church of God that the religious celebration of the Sabbath day should be transferred to 'the Lord's Day.' During the theological controversies of the sixteenth century, Catholic theologians often appealed to the ecclesiastical origin of Sunday in order to prove the power of the Church to introduce new laws and ceremonies. The echo of such a controversy can be detected even in the historical Lutheran Augsburg Confession (1530), which states: 'They [the Catholics] refer to the Sabbath-day as having been changed into the Lord's Day, contrary to the Decalogue [Ten Commandments], as it seems. Neither is there any example whereof they make more than concerning the changing of the Sabbath-day. Great, say they, is the power of the Church, since it has dispensed with one of the Ten Commandments!'"[45] I hope that the reader can see this for exactly what it is – error. No man, system or institution has the authority to change the commandments of YHWH.

The winds of change were blowing from as early as the first and second centuries. In the year 115 AD, Ignatius, the Bishop of Antioch wrote  in a letter to the Magnesians: "If then those who had walked in ancient practices attained unto newness of hope, no longer observing sabbaths but fashioning their lives after the Lord's day, on which our life also arose through Him and through His death which some men deny . . ." While there are various translations of this document they all seem to

infer that there was a new emphasis developing toward Sunday and a diminishment of Sabbath observance. This letter came only decades after the death of the original disciples which dramatically illustrates how quickly error can be perpetrated within organized religious systems. It is also interesting to note that Ignatius was from Antioch a place where the disciples were first called Christians (Acts 11:26) and a culture deeply steeped in paganism and apparently susceptible to false doctrine.[46] In fact, the Temple of Fortuna in Antioch was actually rededicated by Christians for their own use.

By the time that Ignatius wrote his letter, there were numerous problems within the Assembly of Believers including schisms, false doctrines and other heresies. The early faith was pummeled on all sides by critics and deceivers. Shaul spent much of his ministry attempting to correct the problems which festered in the early Assemblies but as soon as the original Disciples passed away, the wolves rushed in like a tidal wave just as had been predicted. (Mattityahu 7:15; Acts 20:29; 2 Timothy 4:3; 2 Kepha 2:1).

The problem worsened over the centuries because many of the well known "Church Fathers" came out of Gnosticism and brought some of their heretical beliefs with them. Epiphanius had been a Nicolaitan, Ambrose of Milan had been a Valentinian and Augustine had been a Manichean for 9 years before joining the Catholic Church.[47] We know very little about the character of these men – only the words which history has recorded concerning them. Sadly, it appears that some of their theology was flawed.

"All of these Gnostic sects were distinguished by their rejection of the Old Testament Law [Torah], some of them even rejecting the Mighty One of the Old Testament [YHWH], and some of them even equated the Mighty One of the Old Testament [YHWH] with the Evil One [hashatan]! In their rejection of the Old Testament Law [Torah], the Valentinian Gnostics even rejected all moral laws, leading to scandalous living. This Valentinianism acted as a half-way house for two hundred years between heathenism and Christianity. The Marcionites were later on refuted, but they also contributed toward the aversion to, and even rejection of, the Old Testament [Tanakh]. Sun-worshipping Mithraism, who advanced Babylonian (Chaldean) astrology with the Sun at the center of it, played a major role in the resultant merger between Sun-worship and the Messianic Belief. Manes and his followers, the Manicheans, from among them Augustine came, 'looked on Judaism with horror, rejected the Old Testament [Tanakh] entirely, and [Manicheism] was not improbably born in an outbreak of anti-Semitic fury.' The Manicheans (who were half-Christians) kept Sunday in honour of the Sun . . ."[48]

The passing of several hundred years saw the decline of Hebrew adherents and the rise of a Gentile dominated religion, very different from the faith and teaching of the Messiah and the Disciples.  During the year 325 C.E. the Roman Catholic Church was birthed at the Council of Nicea. The Council was convened by the Roman Emperor Constantine, an ardent worshipper of the sun god Mithras, who bore the title "Pontifus Maximus" – The

High Priest of Paganism - despite his politically motivated "conversion" to Christianity.[49] The Council was attended by selected "church leaders" which excluded all Hebrew Believers. Various doctrinal issues were debated and agreed upon which resulted in the Nicean Creed. The Council was, in large part, controlled by Eusebius, a Bishop with questionable motives and beliefs.

Constantine's hand picked Council is responsible for outlawing synagogues and the Torah - not a very promising start for a religion that supposedly worshiped a resurrected Hebrew Rabbi that regularly attended the Synagogue where He read and taught the Torah. Prior to the convening of this Council, Constantine had already issued a proclamation on March 7, 321 A.D. stating: *"All judges and city people and the craftsmen shall rest upon the Venerable Day of the Sun."*

The "official" change from Sabbath to Sunday occurred at the Council of Laodicea which took place sometime between 343 and 381 C.E. According to Canon 29: *"Christians must not Judaize by resting on the Sabbath, but must work on that day, rather honouring the Lord's Day; and, if they can, resting then as Christians. But if any shall be found to be Judaizers, let them be shut out from Christ."* This was a very anti-Semitic gathering which issued such other proclamations as forbidding fasting with Jews or receiving unleavened bread from Jews.

The transfer from Sabbath to Sunday seemed inevitable due to the ever increasing pagan influences which poured into the Assembly over the centuries and was eventually consummated thanks to Eusebius and his many followers known as Eusebians.

"Bishop Eusebius (270-338 C.E.), who worked with Constantine, admits the Church's decision to change from Sabbath to Sunday. 'All things whatsoever that it was duty to do on the Sabbath, these we have transferred to the Lord's Day.'"[50]

The Lord's Day, which Christians interpret to be Sunday, has always been a sacred day to sun god worshippers, thus the name Sun Day. Christians hang on one particular verse found in The Book of Revelation to justify the honoring of this day. The passage, written by Yahonatan reads as follows: *I came to be in the Spirit on the Day of YHWH.* Many English Bibles translate the "Day of YHWH" as "the Lord's Day" which has no particular meaning in the context of the Scriptures. The "Day of YHWH" on the other hand is a specific Day mentioned within the Scriptures at least 30 times and referred to in 300 similar terms.

Thus "The Day" that Yahonatan was referring to was the "Day of YHWH" not some vague new day called "the Lord's Day" and this passage in no way may be used to support the notion that the Sabbath was changed to Sun Day. "The first day of each week, Sunday, was consecrated to Mithra since times remote . . . [b]ecause the Sun was god, the Lord par excellence, Sunday came to be called the Lord's day, as later was done by Christianity."[51]

I have no dispute with the fact that Sunday is considered to be "the Lord's day". Since "baal" means "lord" in Hebrew, the fact that Sun Day was the traditional day of the week that sun god worshippers revered their "lord" it is quite fitting. This point demonstrates the problem with using titles instead of names in

our worship. Sun worshippers are referring to Baal, Mithra, Rha, Jupiter, Zeus, Helios, Attis, Tammuz, Osiris and the like when they say "lord" while Christians use the same title when referring to their Savior. Both use the same title and worship on the same day which poses quite a dilemma for Christians, especially when the Creator of the Universe calls the seventh day Sabbath set apart.

The stage had been set for the change from Sabbath to Sunday by two previous edicts issued by Constantine. The first was called the Edict of Milan and was issued in 313 C.E. which adopted a policy of universal religious freedom and ended the persecution of Christians. The second was called the Edict of Constantine and was issued in the year 321 C.E. This edict legislated the venerable day of the Sun (Sunday) to be a rest day. This act was in perfect harmony with Constantine's renowned and continuing involvement in sun god worship.

In 341 C.E. at the Council of Antioch, Christians were forbidden from celebrating the Passover which is one of the Appointed Times (moadi) commanded in the Scriptures (Vayiqra 23). Instead, Christians were instructed to celebrate Easter, a day rooted in pagan worship and named after the fertility goddess Easter, also known as Astarte. Thus the reason for dyed eggs which were traditionally dipped in the blood of sacrificed infants on the altar of Easter.  Many other pagan traditions were incorporated into the Christian celebration of Easter.

Since many early Christian converts grew up in a pagan society and were probably pagans, they likely

considered Sunday to be a special day all of their lives. The Council's decision to replace the unfamiliar seventh day Sabbath with the well-known "Lord's Day" was most likely met with favor. It fit in well with people's habits and traditions. By observing the first day of the week (Sunday) as a sabbath instead of seventh day of the week, pagan converts did not have to change their shopping routine or upset their weekly work schedule. They could continue going to the mall, mowing their lawns and working on their favorite home improvement projects on Saturday, just as they had when they were pagans.

One group of Believers that would have been manifestly opposed to such a change was the Nazarenes who, by that time, were few in numbers and generally not affiliated with the now mainstream anti-nomian Gentile dominated Christian "Church."[52] In fact, due to growing anti-Semitic sentiment within the Christian "Church" and the friction that existed between Torah observant Believers and generally lawless Christians, the change was probably welcomed by many Christians because it brought about a long overdue separation from something considered to be "Jewish".

This sentiment is noticeably expressed in the writings of early Christian historians such as Epiphanius

 who wrote the following: "They [the Nazarenes] have no different ideas, but confess everything exactly as the Law proclaims it and in the Jewish fashion - except for their belief in Messiah . . . but since they are still fettered by the Law - circumcision, the Sabbath, and the rest - they are not in accord with Christians." *Panarion 29.*

Notice how he tries to portray the Nazarenes as heretics, but the only accusation that he has against them is that they obey the commandments as opposed to Christians, who do not. Sadly, that same attitude exists to this day. Most Catholic and Christian adherents believe that the seventh day Sabbath is strictly a "Jewish" observance so they regularly profane the Sabbath and then criticize anyone who observes the Sabbath as putting themselves "under the law".

Shaul coined this phrase which, like many of his other writings, has been twisted by dispensationalist thinkers to meet their ends – in this case the end of the Torah. Obeying the commandments does not put one "under the law" unless you are relying on that obedience to save your soul, which it cannot do. If, on the other hand, you have been saved by grace, then your reasonable service is to love your Master with all your heart and with all your soul (Devarim 6:5) which will lead to a desire to obey Him with all your heart and with all your soul (Devarim 26:16).

This is exactly what the Messiah taught His disciples (Mattityahu 22:37). He wants His disciples to love <u>and</u> obey which brings about a complete obedience on the inside and the outside. He often chastised the Pharisees because they were teaching His people but they were hypocrites - they taught one thing and did another. They obeyed on the outside but their hearts were corrupt. He put it very bluntly when He said: "²⁷ Woe to you, teachers of the law and Pharisees, you hypocrites! You are like whitewashed tombs, which look beautiful on the outside but on the inside are full of dead men's bones and everything unclean. ²⁸ In the same way, on the outside you appear to people as righteous but on the inside you are full of hypocrisy and wickedness." Mattityahu

23:27-28 NIV.

He clearly taught that He expected His followers to obey the Torah as we read in the following teaching: "*²⁷ You have heard that it was said, 'Do not commit adultery.'* ²⁸ *But I tell you that anyone who looks at a woman lustfully has already committed adultery with her in his heart.*" Mattityahu 5:27-29 NIV. He instructed His followers not to commit adultery with their bodies <u>and</u> not to commit adultery in their hearts (Shemot 20:14; Mattityahu 5:27-28). This is true Torah teaching.

Again the Messiah taught: "*²¹ You have heard that it was said to the people long ago, 'Do not murder, and anyone who murders will be subject to judgment.' ²² But I tell you that anyone who is angry with his brother will be subject to judgment.*" Mattityahu 5:21-22 NIV. Again He is instructing people to obey, not just with their bodies, but in their hearts as well. This is the complete obedience that YHWH has always desired from His people and in no way abolishes the Torah. To the contrary it is the fulfillment of the Torah as the Messiah said He came to do (Mattityahu 5:17).

The Catholic and Christian religious systems have rejected the teaching of the Messiah because they have rejected His Torah. They teach against the commandments and proclaim that they are abolished. As a result, they are lawless religions that teach their own rules and traditions rather than the commandments of YHWH. The sad part is that most do not realize that this is what they are doing because they have inherited lies from the fathers of their religion – men like Epiphanius who criticized the Early Believers for observing the Sabbath (Yirmeyahu 16:9).

Catholic leaders and historians make no bones about the fact that the Scriptural Sabbath is the seventh day and

it was the Catholic Church which altered the Sabbath within their religious system. According to one Catholic Catechism: "Saturday is the Sabbath . . . We observe Sunday instead of Saturday because the Catholic Church transferred the solemnity from Saturday to Sunday."[53]

James Cardinal Gibbons, a prominent Catholic Authority on this subject and former Archbishop of Baltimore affirmed this fact by stating: "The Catholic Church . . . by virtue of her divine mission, changed the day from Saturday to Sunday." He further stated that "you may read the Bible from Genesis to Revelation, and you will not find a single line authorizing the sanctification of Sunday. The Scriptures enforce the religious observance of Saturday, a day  which we never sanctify."[54] On November 11, 1895 the Office of Cardinal Gibbons through Chancellor H.F. Thomas stated: "Of course the Catholic Church claims that the change was her act . . . and *the act is a mark* of her ecclesiastical power." This change is repeatedly referred to as a mark. "*Sunday is our mark of authority!* . . The Church is, above the Bible, and this transference of Sabbath observance is proof of that fact."[55]

We have already seen that the Sabbath is a sign or distinguishing mark for those who follow YHWH, now we see that the Catholic Church deems Sunday worship as her mark. This should be disconcerting to anyone familiar with the Prophet Daniel who wrote that the Anti-Messiah, often referred to as the Anti-Christ, will ". . . *speak words against the Most High [God] and shall wear out the saints of the Most High and think to change the time [of sacred feasts and holy*

days] and the law . . ." Daniel 7:25 AMP (See also Revelation 13).

There is no doubt that: "Sunday is a Catholic institution, and its claims to observance can be defended only on Catholic principles."[56] The Catholic Church used the Sabbath issue as proof that it is the "True Church" because it demonstrates her power to change the commandments of YHWH. "Had she not such power, she could not have done that in which all modern religionists agree with her – She could not have substituted the observance of Sunday the first day of the week, for the observance of Saturday the seventh day, a change for which there is no Scriptural authority."[57]

Catholics are even baffled by Protestants, who allegedly "protested" against the authority of the Catholic Church, yet continue to follow Catholic dogma over the express commands found within the Scriptures. "It is well to remind the Presbyterians, Baptists, Methodists, and all other Christians, that the Bible does not support them anywhere in their observance of Sunday. Sunday is an institution of the Roman Catholic Church, and those who observe the day observe a commandment of the Catholic Church."[58]

"Protestants, who accept the Bible as the only rule of faith and religion, should by all means go back to the observance of the Sabbath. The fact that they do not, but on the contrary observe the Sunday, stultifies them in the eyes of every thinking man . . . We Catholics do not accept the Bible as the only rule of faith. Besides the Bible we have the living Church, the authority of the Church, as a rule to guide us. We say, this Church, instituted by Christ to teach and guide man through life, has the right to change

ceremonial laws of the Old Testament and hence, we accept her change of the Sabbath to Sunday. . . It is always somewhat laughable, to see the Protestant churches, in pulpit legislation, demand the observance of Sunday, of which there is nothing in the Bible."[59]

The Catholics are very clear on this issue. "If you follow the Bible alone there can be no question that you are obliged to keep Saturday holy, since that is the day especially prescribed by Almighty God to be kept holy to the Lord."[60] Catholics acknowledge that the Scriptures command a seventh day Sabbath and only if you believe that the Catholic Church has the power to change the Scriptures should you recognize and observe Sunday – The Lord's Day.

12

Protestant Christianity and the Sabbath

Thus far it has been demonstrated how important the Sabbath is to YHWH and we have seen that Yahushua obeyed the Sabbath and taught concerning the Sabbath as did Shaul. Despite the irrefutable fact that the Catholic Church changed their Sabbath to Sunday, there are still many Christians who believe that the Sabbath was supernaturally changed from the last day of the week to the first day of the week by Yahushua. As was previously mentioned, part of this misunderstanding is based upon the mistaken belief that Yahushua was resurrected on Easter Sunday – which He was not.

Aside from that, if Yahushua had come to abolish or change one of the most significant commandments found in the Scriptures, one would think that there would be at least one reference where He revealed His intentions to do so. Instead, all of His teachings on the Sabbath were based upon the Torah and were intended to direct men to the real purpose of the Sabbath.

There is not one Scripture passage that indicates that the Sabbath was changed from the seventh day of the week to the first day of the week. If Yahushua was going to change the Fourth Commandment, He would have explicitly said so. Instead what He said was: *"¹⁷ Do not think*

that I came to destroy the Law (Torah) or the prophets. I did not come to destroy but to fulfill (complete). [18] *For assuredly, I say to you, till heaven and earth pass away, one jot or one tittle will by no means pass from the Torah till all is fulfilled (completed)."* Mattithyahu 5:17-18. He also said that *"it is easier for the heaven and the earth to pass away than for one tittle of the Torah to fall."* Luke 16:17.[61]

The teaching that the Sabbath was replaced by Sunday worship is a lie which has been inherited and most people never even question the truth or the origin of the teaching. I recall pondering this problem in Christianity as a youth, but never getting a clear answer. I also remember one fine Preacher from an old country church that I attended questioning this contradiction during a Sunday morning service, but ultimately tradition won out over the plain truth of the Scriptures. I remember the frustration in his voice as he resigned himself to the fact that nothing he said would change the momentum created by centuries of Sunday observance.

This is exactly what satan (hashatan), the adversary, is counting on. As already mentioned, the prophesied anti-messiah desires to change the appointed times of YHWH and set up his own world political, economic and religious system. The attempted abolition of the Sabbath and the convergence of the "Christian Sabbath" with Sun Day, a day pagans devote to sun god worship, is no coincidence. Sun worship has been around since the days of Noah and it is practiced in most cultures under different names and through different gods. At the core though it is all the same and the goal is to lead people away from the Almighty and into false worship.

Time is the adversary's best friend and his worst enemy. Time allows him to imbed his false doctrines, traditions and customs slowly and steadily into organized religion so that adherents ultimately do not see the abomination which is staring them in the face. His desire is to lead people away from the Torah, away from a life of obedience and into a state of lawlessness, which is the path of destruction. According to Shaul, the secret power of lawlessness was at work even while he was alive (2 Thessalonians 2:7). It is now *time* for followers of YHWH to shake off the lies which they have inherited and begin to walk in truth before it is too late.

I realize that this message may be shocking to many Christians who have spent their entire lives profaning the Sabbath, thinking that Sunday was the "Christian Sabbath", but you do not have to take my word alone. In fact, many well known and highly regarded Protestant teachers have long recognized the truth, but have been equally unsuccessful in their efforts to reform their respective denominations. Read what some have written concerning the Sabbath:

- "Some say, it was changed from the seventh to the first day. Where? When? And by whom? No man can tell. No; it was never changed, nor could it be, unless creation was to be gone through again: for the reason assigned must be changed before the observance, or respect to the reason, can be changed! It is all old wives' fables to talk of the change of the Sabbath from the seventh to the first day. If it be changed, it was that august personage changed it who changes

times and laws ex officio – I think his name is Doctor Antichrist." [62]

- "They err in teaching that Sunday has taken the place of the Old Testament Sabbath and therefore must be kept as the seventh day had to be kept by the children of Israel . . . These churches err in their teaching, for Scripture has in no way ordained the first day of the week in place of the Sabbath. There is simply no law in the New Testament to that effect."[63]

- "The moral law contained in the ten commandments, and enforced by the prophets, He [Messiah] did not take away. It was not the design of His coming to revoke any part of this. This is a law which never can be broken . . . Every part of this law must remain in force upon all mankind, and in all ages; as not depending either on time or place, or any other circumstances liable to change . . ."[64]

- "The Sabbath was binding in Eden, and it has been in force ever since . . . How can men claim that this one commandment has been done away with when they will admit that the other nine are still binding?"[65]

- "The Sabbath is a part of the Decalogue – the Ten Commandments. This alone forever settles the question as to the perpetuity of the institution . . . Until, therefore, it can be shown that the whole moral law has been repealed, the Sabbath will stand."[66]

- "[I]t is quite clear that however rigidly or devotedly we may spend Sunday, we are not

keeping the Sabbath . . . [which] was founded on a specific Divine command. We can plead no such command for the obligation to observe Sunday . . . There is not a single sentence in the New Testament to suggest that we incur any penalty by violating the supposed sanctity of Sunday."[67]

If this is not enough I would encourage every person to conduct their own research of the Scriptures and locate every passage which speaks of honoring and obeying the Sabbath or the importance of the Sabbath. Then locate every passage which speaks of changing or nullifying the Sabbath. You can do the work yourself or you can rely upon my calculations. I located 160 passages of Scripture which speak of keeping the weekly Sabbath and I did not find any Scriptures which spoke of changing or nullifying the Sabbath, observing Sunday as the Sabbath or making every day a Sabbath. Of course, this was not surprising to me since YHWH does not change. (Malachi 3:6).

Therefore, if Protestant Christians profess to worship the Almighty, then they should observe the Sabbath as a sign or mark in their lives rather that the mark of the Roman Catholic Church.

13

Blessings and Curses

Sabbath observance is often a divisive issue because people fail to understand the operation of Torah and grace. Some erroneously believe that because a person is saved by grace they no longer should follow Torah. Nothing could be farther from the truth. Our walk with YHWH requires us to live righteously and we still find His instruction for righteous living within the Torah.

As with many of the commandments we may not always see the exact reason for obeying, but it comes down to whether or not we believe and trust YHWH. Just as a person may initially be saved by simple childlike faith, they are expected to learn and grow and live out that faith. All of these aspects of faith involve believing the promises and truth found within the Scriptures. This is also the case with Sabbath observance. At first you may not understand the reason for observing Shabbat. All you need to know is that it is a commandment which must be obeyed. Over time, through your simple obedience you will begin to see the purpose – it will become obvious.

How many times have you as a parent said, or as a child heard the following: "Never mind why, just do as I say." The parent knows why they are commanding the child to do something, but the child does not always

understand the purpose. The child wants to know the parent's reasoning, but because the child is not old enough to understand or comprehend, the parent desires for the child to simply trust him or her. The parent's motivation is in the child's best interests, but the parent does not always have to thoroughly explain his or her reasoning. So it is with our Heavenly Father. He has given us instructions which we sometimes fail to understand. We may not always have an adequate explanation for His purpose and must simply obey and trust because by doing so we are blessed.

The words of the prophet Yeshayahu on this subject are clear: "*Blessed is the man who does this, and the son of man who lays hold on it; who keeps from defiling the Sabbath, and keeps his hand from doing any evil.*" Yeshayahu 56:2. There are numerous blessings outlined in the Scriptures for obeying the commandments in general, which include the Sabbath. (Devarim 7:12-16; 28:1-14; Vayiqra 26:1-13). Interestingly, some of the blessings include physical blessings, a fact which has been supported by science.

Read what one person has to say about the health benefits of observing the Sabbath. "God built a need for rest into the very fabric of our selves. If we ignore it, we get sick. All work and no play makes us dull, listless, and restless. We become impatient, angry, neurotic, and distressed. We feel time-driven and obsessed with productivity. Sabbath rest can also fill us with tranquility in the midst of oppressive situations. If you wonder where all your stress (and perhaps your depression) is coming from, consider the balance of your life. Sabbath rest is the best anti-depressant and anti-anxiety prescription available. Proverbs 14 says, 'A tranquil mind gives life to the flesh,

but passion makes the bones rot' (v. 30). Sabbath rest is the key to tranquility. The word *tranquil* comes from the Latin words *trans* (beyond) and *quillus* (quiet). A tranquil person is free from outside agitation and ruled with a calmness from beyond that 'gives life to the flesh.' Conversely, wrong passion 'makes the bones rot.' It makes life fall into disarray and become wasted. Wrong passion is all work and no play, all labor and no worship, all self and no Christ. By keeping Sabbath we can achieve a state of uprooted passions and reintegrated passion for Christ - a deep inner tranquility sustained by watchful prayer. For your health's sake, keep the Sabbath. As a person more in tune with God, you will live better and be better!"[68]

There are also curses associated with not keeping the Sabbath and the punishment for disobedience is severe. Read what YHWH said to Mosheh: *"[13] Speak also to the children of Yisra'el, saying: 'Surely My Sabbaths you shall keep, for it is a sign between Me and you throughout your generations, that you may know that I am YHWH who sanctifies you. [14] You shall keep the Sabbath, therefore, for it is holy to you. Everyone who profanes it shall surely be put to death; for whoever does any work on it, that person shall be cut off from among his people.[15] Work shall be done for six days, but the seventh is the Sabbath of rest, holy to YHWH. Whoever does any work on the Sabbath day, he shall surely be put to death. [16] Therefore the children of Yisra'el shall keep the Sabbath, to observe the Sabbath throughout their generations as a perpetual covenant. [17] It is a sign between Me and the children of Yisra'el forever; for in six days YHWH made the heavens and the earth, and on the seventh day He rested and was refreshed.'"* Shemot 31:13-17.

Notice that in one passage, the death penalty is cited twice for profaning the Sabbath. Repeating something is

one way in which the Scriptures emphasize the importance of a particular issue. The Scriptures recount an example when the death sentence was actually executed against an individual for profaning the Sabbath. *"32 While the Yisra'elites were in the desert, a man was found gathering wood on the Sabbath day. 33 Those who found him gathering wood brought him to Mosheh and Aharon and the whole assembly, 34 and they kept him in custody, because it was not clear what should be done to him. 35 Then YHWH said to Mosheh, 'The man must die. The whole assembly must stone him outside the camp.' 36 So the assembly took him outside the camp and stoned him to death, as YHWH commanded Mosheh."* Bemidbar 15:32-36.

Make no mistake, this was no accident. The man was willfully, intentionally and belligerently disobeying YHWH in the presence of the assembly. While the penalty may seem severe for gathering sticks, it displays the expectation that YHWH has for those who are a part of His Assembly. If you do not like the rules or desire to disobey them, you cannot dwell in the camp with Elohim and His people.

The prophet Yirmeyahu gave a stern warning to Yisra'el regarding the Sabbath:

> *21 This is what YHWH says: Be careful not to carry a load on the Sabbath day or bring it through the gates of Yahrushalayim. 22 Do not bring a load out of your houses or do any work on the Sabbath, but keep the Sabbath day set apart, as I commanded your forefathers. 23 Yet they did not listen or pay attention; they were stiff-necked and would not listen or respond to discipline. 24 But if you are careful to obey me, declares YHWH, and bring no load through the gates of*

this city on the Sabbath, but keep the Sabbath day set apart by not doing any work on it, ²⁵ then kings who sit on Dawid's throne will come through the gates of this city with their officials. They and their officials will come riding in chariots and on horses, accompanied by the men of Yahudah and those living in Yahrushalayim, and this city will be inhabited forever. ²⁶ People will come from the towns of Yahudah and the villages around Yahrushalayim, from the territory of Binyamin and the western foothills, from the hill country and the Negev, bringing burnt offerings and slaughter offerings, grain offerings, incense and thank offerings to the house of YHWH. ²⁷ But if you do not obey me to keep the Sabbath day set apart by not carrying any load as you come through the gates of Yahrushalayim on the Sabbath day, then I will kindle an unquenchable fire in the gates of Yahrushalayim that will consume her fortresses. Yirmeyahu 17:21-27.

As you can see, the Sabbath is serious business to YHWH: penalties for disobedience amount to death and destruction. It was also the reason why Yahudah was expelled from the land, because they failed give the land its' Sabbath rest. *"The land enjoyed its Sabbath rests; all the time of its desolation it rested, until the seventy years were completed in fulfillment of the word of YHWH spoken by Yirmeyahu."* 2 Chronicles (Dibre ha Yamin) 36:21. In the end, the land still rested which shows that it is better just to obey and receive the blessings than to disobey and receive punishment.

Imagine what it means to give the land rest for an entire year. The residual blessing is that men, women and

animals would not have to toil in the fields for an entire year. What a blessing and what a lesson in faith. At first, it seems hard to believe that the children of Yisra'el would not obey this command but all you have to do is examine most people during a week long period to understand the problem. If people cannot even rest for one day out of the week, how will they ever obey the command concerning the Sabbath rest for the land.

The prophet Ezekiel (Yehezqel)[69] also shows how profaning the Sabbath was a reason for Yisra'el being scattered throughout the world. "*[18] But I said to their children in the wilderness, 'Do not walk in the statutes of your fathers, nor observe their judgments, nor defile yourselves with their idols.[19] I am YHWH your Elohim: Walk in My statutes, keep My judgments, and do them; [20] set apart My Sabbaths, and they will be a sign between Me and you, that you may know that I am YHWH your Elohim.' [21] Notwithstanding, the children rebelled against Me; they did not walk in My statutes, and were not careful to observe My judgments, which, if a man does, he shall live by them; but they profaned My Sabbaths. Then I said I would pour out My fury on them and fulfill My anger against them in the wilderness.[22] Nevertheless I withdrew My Hand and acted for My Name's sake, that it should not be profaned in the sight of the Gentiles, in whose sight I had brought them out.[23] Also I raised My hand in an oath to those in the wilderness, that I would scatter them among the Gentiles and disperse them throughout the countries, [24] because they had not executed My judgments, but had despised My statutes, profaned My Sabbaths, and their eyes were fixed on their fathers' idols."* Yehezqel 20:18-24. It is clear from this prophesy that failure to obey the Sabbath is considered rebellion and profaning the Sabbath results in punishment.

This begs the question: Why would YHWH place

such an emphasis on the Sabbath Day and exert such severe punishment of His children for profaning the Sabbath if He only planned on changing the day. The answer is simple: YHWH does not change. (Malachi 3:6). YHWH has an eternal plan for His Sabbath. He provides blessings for those who obey and curses for those who choose to disobey: the choice is yours.

14

Conclusion

With all of the severe punishments associated with profaning the Sabbath, the only way that Christians can justify their perpetual state of disobedience is to somehow explain away the significance of the Sabbath. I have heard some Christians make the profound statement that they do not observe the seventh day as the Sabbath because: "every day is a Sabbath." They make this statement because this is what they have been taught, but there is simply no foundation or truth to this belief. If that statement were correct, then nobody would ever get any work done because we are not supposed to work on the Sabbath. If every day were the Sabbath, then you would have to rest every day.

This is a false doctrine which traces back to Justin Martyr who in his Dialogue with Trypho ridiculed the Yahudim for observing the weekly Sabbath by stating: "and you, because you are idle for one day, suppose you are pious." According to Justin "the new law requires you to keep perpetual Sabbath." Justin was a philosopher of Plato who converted to Christianity and later considered himself to be a Christian philosopher. He maintained that the two schools of thought were in many ways compatible and his teachings are heavily influenced

by Greek philosophy.

    Confusion concerning the Sabbath also derives from a mistaken belief that the Sabbath is simply about which day of the week we worship, which it is not. The Sabbath is primarily about rest and communion with YHWH and He never gave permission to any man to work on this set apart day. In fact, He led by example: He rested. The Sabbath was never designated for common labor and there is no mention in the New Testament about the Sabbath being abolished, changed or anything of the kind. The Sabbath is mentioned in the New Testament fifty-nine times, and always with the same importance that it had in the Tanakh.

    It is plain to see that the Sabbath is very significant and applicable to all that call upon the Name of YHWH. He set this day apart, not as a burden, but as a time of freedom to worship Him and seek His face without any stresses or concerns which we experience in our normal daily routines. The Sabbath is not meant to be ordinary, it is special and there is nobody on earth who can say that they did not have time for YHWH because He made the time for us. When you begin to truly treat the Sabbath as a set apart day and recognize its' significance, you will begin to experience incredible blessings.

    Ultimately, Yahushua *"has become the High Priest forever, in the order of Melchizedek."* (Ibrim 6:20) and as High Priest, He offers His own blood which is able to *"cleanse our consciences from acts that lead to death, so that we may serve the living Elohim!"* Ibrim 9:14. If you are a follower of Yahushua, then you are a priest according to the order of Melchizedek (Revelation 1:6; 1 Kepha 2:9). Priests must learn to distinguish between the set apart (qadosh) and the profane.

Read what the prophet Yehezqel prophesied regarding the wicked leaders of Yisra'el. *"Her priests have violated My Torah and profaned My set apart things; they have not distinguished between the set apart and profane, nor have they made known the difference between the unclean and the clean; and they have hidden their eyes from My Sabbaths, so that I am profaned among them."* Yehezqel 22:26.

Notice from this passage that YHWH Himself is profaned among them because the priests did not distinguish between the set apart and the profane, they did not make known the difference between the clean and the unclean and they hid their eyes from YHWH's Sabbaths. The death and resurrection of the Messiah did not change these important distinctions. If you want to serve as a priest you must get clean and stay clean. If you intentionally disregard the commandments of YHWH, including profaning the Sabbath, you will be disqualified from service.

Regrettably, I have heard some Christian teachers and preachers speak with disdain about "Sabbath-keepers". They ignorantly preach that those who honor the Sabbath are putting themselves "under the law" and falling "into bondage."[70] I anguish for these false teachers because their future holds a certain expectation of judgment based upon the following statement of Yahushua: *"Whoever therefore breaks one of the least of these commandments, and teaches men so, shall be called least in the kingdom of heaven."* Mattityahu 5:19 NKJV.

Teachers bear a great responsibility and they owe it to themselves and to those they teach to get it right. That is why Ya'akov declared, *"My brethren, let not many of you become teachers, knowing that we shall receive a stricter*

judgment." Ya'akov 3:1 NKJV. I cannot imagine what that day will be like when so many teachers and preachers will stand before Yahushua and attempt to explain why they mislead His flock and pointed His sheep away from His Torah and His express commandments. I am certain that they will try to tell of all the wonderful deeds that they did in "His Name" but that will not be sufficient (Mattityahu 7:21-23). What a fearful and dreadful day that will be for many (Ibrim 10:31).

In that vein, let us look at a passage from Vayiqra which provides direction regarding certain matters, including the Sabbath, and determine how the typical Christian teacher would respond regarding those matters. "*29 Do not prostitute your daughter, to cause her to be a harlot, lest the land fall into harlotry, and the land become full of wickedness. 30 You shall keep My Sabbaths and reverence My sanctuary: I am YHWH. 31 Give no regard to mediums and familiar spirits; do not seek after them, to be defiled by them: I am YHWH your Elohim. 32 Rise in the presence of the aged, show respect for the elderly and revere your Elohim. I am YHWH.*" Vayiqra 19:29-32.

These passages from the Torah provide instruction on a variety of issues: 1) giving your child into prostitution; 2) keeping the Sabbath and reverencing the sanctuary; 3) avoiding mediums and spiritists; and 4) honoring the elderly. If you asked a Christian teacher whether we should obey the commandment which instructs us not to give our children into prostitution, the answer would no doubt be: "yes". If you asked a Christian teacher whether we should obey the commandment that instructs us to avoid mediums and spiritists, the answer would no doubt be: "yes". If you asked a Christian teacher whether we should obey the

commandment which instructs us to honor the elderly, the answer would no doubt be: "yes".

Interestingly, if you asked a Christian teacher whether we should obey the instruction concerning the Sabbath, the answer would not be so straightforward. You might get answers such as "no" or "the Sabbath is for the Jews" or "the Sabbath was changed" or "we are not under the Law". I could go on and on demonstrating that the Torah gives very basic and beneficial instructions for righteous living and is not a burden but I will not beleaguer the point. I hope that this example demonstrates how utterly inconsistent and illogical Christianity is on the subject of the Sabbath.

Whether you choose to recognize the Sabbath does not change the fact that it still exists and each will give an account in the end concerning their attitude and their treatment of the Sabbath. Once you discover the truth concerning the Sabbath, your response is critical. If you are guilty of profaning the Sabbath, it is important that you repent and then obey the commandments by observing the Sabbath. There is nothing that you can do about the fact that you have been deceived your entire life. The important thing is that you demonstrate that you have a heart to obey once you are shown the truth.

Sabbath observance is simply a matter of obedience, it is not legalism in the negative sense that most Christians try to portray it. If you observe it like Judaism observes it with hundreds of rules and regulations then you have fallen into legalism. If, on the other hand, you follow the simple commands found within the Scriptures, then you are simply being an obedient servant. To equate obedience with bondage or unhealthy legalism is simply foolish and

reflects an immature understanding of the Creator.

Observing the Sabbath is a demonstration of your belief and faith in the True Elohim – the One Who Made the Sabbath. It signifies that you believe in the Creator of the Universe and that you believe His Word. By honoring the Sabbath you honor YHWH and, in this day and age, it sets you apart from the rest of the world that profanes the Sabbath. It shows that you serve, obey and follow the Creator of the Universe, who also rested on that day.

Observing the Sabbath also demonstrates that we believe His promises and that we trust Him. Many times we are so busy and we have so many things to get done it seems impossible to set aside all of our obligations and desires for one day, especially Saturday. In America, and most westernized cultures, everything is open on Saturday and many activities are scheduled for Saturday. It is the nationally recognized "fun" day when we get to do what we want after a busy week of work.

Because of our habits and traditions it is not always easy to refrain from our activities and rest on Shabbat. Some of us have so much work to do that we cannot imagine taking an entire day to do nothing – How unproductive! Yet this is exactly what YHWH expects from us. That is why He emphasized to the Yisra'elites: *"six days you shall labor, but on the seventh day you shall rest; even during the plowing season and harvest you must rest."* Shemot 34:21. In other words, even in their peak season, the most important time of the year they must still set aside all of their work and observe the Sabbath.

By observing the Sabbath we are displaying a willingness to put the commands and concerns of YHWH above our own selfish interests or the interests of our

family or friends. In essence, the Sabbath is a weekly test of our heart toward YHWH. It is a gauge which demonstrates where we stand before Him. The spectrum of this gauge ranges from a complete, knowing and willful rejection of the Sabbath, which results in curses, separation and death, to an absolute reverence for the Sabbath, a submission to the will of YHWH and an immersion in His presence on His set apart day, which results in blessings and life.[71] The choice seems easy to me. We should each examine our own lives and prayerfully consider any necessary changes which must be made to move us closer to Him and His will.

The Sabbath was meant to be a blessing to every Believer and their families. It brings us closer together with our Creator, our family and there are even health benefits associated with resting on the Sabbath.[72] It is not a burden, it is truly freedom. When I first started to observe the Sabbath, it was not always easy but as I continued to obey I began to look forward to the day with anxious anticipation because I knew that blessings awaited me. I encourage each and every reader to begin to obey so that you too can learn the importance of this day and the blessings associated with keeping this commandment (mitzvot).

Read what the prophet Yeshayahu has to say about the true meaning and purpose of Shabbat. "[13] *If you turn away your foot from the Sabbath, from doing your pleasure on My set apart day, and call the Sabbath a delight, the set apart day of YHWH honorable, and shall honor Him, not doing your own ways, nor finding your own pleasure, nor speaking your own words, [14] Then you shall delight yourself in YHWH; and I will cause you to ride on the high hills of the earth, and feed you with the heritage of Ya'akov your father. The mouth of YHWH has spoken.*" Yeshayahu 58:13-14. Can you see what

YHWH has in store for those who worship Him in spirit and in truth and for those who obey Him in spirit and in truth - it is all good.

It is important to reiterate that the Torah was *not* given to slaves, it was given to free people and it was meant for free people. In fact, the commandment regarding the Sabbath specifically states *"And remember that you were a slave in the land of Mitsrayim, and YHWH your Elohim brought you out from there by a mighty hand and by an outstretched arm; therefore YHWH your Elohim commanded you to keep the Sabbath day."* Devarim 5:15. We are reminded of the past slavery of Yisra'el as we keep the Sabbath as free people. The Yisra'elites were not permitted to observe the Sabbath when they were slaves. In other words: They were not free to obey. The question that I pose to the reader is this: Are you free to obey or are you a slave to your family, cultural or religious customs or traditions which prohibit you from being obedient? The Sabbath is a gift from YHWH to a people who have been freed from bondage.

The bottom line is that those who believe that the Sabbath was changed to Sunday rarely correctly observe Sunday as a Sabbath. Most likely, they continue to cook, buy, sell and perform household chores, among other things. While they may attend a worship service, that is not, in itself, proper Sabbath observance. The Sabbath was never changed by YHWH, only by men who erroneously claim to have the authority to alter His commandments. No man or institution has such authority and it is time for Christians to admit that they have inherited lies, worthlessness and unprofitable things. (Yirmeyahu 16:19-20).

Countless Christians have been misled regarding the Sabbath who now need to readjust their thinking and behavior. Sabbath observance is a sign to the world that you are one of the Redeemed who are set apart to YHWH and hold fast to His covenant. It provides rest, renewal, refreshing and communion with YHWH and it is a continuing and integral part of the renewed covenant ushered in by Yahushua the Messiah. Therefore, if you want to be part of that covenant then the Sabbath needs to be part of you. Shabbat Shalom!

Endnotes

[1] Dispensationalism in its most recent popular form derived primarily from the Bible School movement in the United States and the Scofield Bible. Dispensationalism promotes the replacement of the "old" with the "new". It teaches that the "church" has replaced Yisra'el and that grace has replaced the "law" among other things. This doctrine has no support in the Scriptures and is merely a way for men to explain the changes which have occurred within Christianity over the past two thousand years. It is a very dangerous doctrine which has pervaded most of modern Christianity. I call it dangerous because it completely distorts the plan of the Creator of the Universe as described in the Scriptures and actually alters the way that people read the Scriptures. It justifies lawlessness by advocating the abolishment of the commandments. It teaches that the commandments were only for the "Jews" leaving Christianity in a quandary because the Messiah Who is the "Word That Became Flesh" obeyed the commandments and instructed those who loved Him to obey His commandments which are not just to love one another as is commonly taught. (John 14). In fact, He specifically stated that He did not come to abolish the "Law". (Matthew 5:17). Dispensationalism is discussed in greater detail in the Walk in the Light series book entitled "The Law and Grace".

[2] YHWH is the English translation of the Hebrew tetragrammaton (יהוה) which is the Name of the Creator of the Universe. A detailed discussion of the Name is found in the Walk in the Light Series book entitled "Names".

[3] Elohim (אלהים) is the proper Hebrew word which is often translated "God" and refers to the Creator of the Universe described in the Hebrew and Christian Scriptures.

[4] The Torah (תורה) is the first five books of the Hebrew and Christian Scriptures. It was written by Moses (Mosheh) and is often referred to as "The Law" in many modern English Bibles . Law is a very harsh, cold word which often results in the Torah being confused with the laws, customs and traditions of the religious leaders as well as the laws of particular countries. The

Torah is more accurately defined as the "instruction" of YHWH for His set apart people. The Torah contains instruction for those who desire to live righteous, set apart lives in accordance with the will of YHWH. Contrary to popular belief, people can obey the Torah. (Devarim 30:11-14). It is the myriads of regulations, customs and traditions which men attach to the Torah that make it impossible and burdensome for people to obey. The names of the five different "books" are transliterated from their proper Hebrew names as follows: Genesis - Beresheet, Exodus - Shemot, Leviticus - Vayiqra, Numbers - Bemidbar, Deuteronomy - Devarim.

5 Mosheh (מֹשֶׁה) is the proper transliteration for the name of the Patriarch commonly called Moses.

6 The use of the word "old" to describe the Torah and other writings has bolstered the doctrines of men such as Marcion who taught that the "God" of the "Old Testament" is different than the "God" of the "New Testament". The impression given is that the "new" is better than the "old" and that the "new" has even replaced the "old". This is a very dangerous teaching and needless to say - false. To avoid the problems associated with this "old" versus "new" contradiction, I use the customary Hebrew acronym Tanakh when referring specifically to "Old Testament" Scriptures and I use Messianic Scriptures when referring specifically to "New Testament" Scriptures. The Tanakh consists of the T̲orah (Five Books of Mosheh), N̲ebi'im (Prophets) and the K̲ethubim (Writings), thus the acronym TNK which is pronounced tah-nach. While much, if not all, of the Tanakh deals with the Messiah in one way or another, the Messianic Scriptures specifically detail the ministry of the Messiah and therefore I think that, while not perfect, it gets the point across in a more meaningful way. For a deeper discussion on this issue see the Walk in the Light Series book entitled "The Scriptures".

7 Yisra'el is the English transliteration for the Hebrew word יִשְׂרָאֵל often spelled Israel.

8 Egypt is the modern word used to describe the land inhabited by the descendents of Mitsrayim, who was the son of Ham (Beresheet 10:6). Thus, throughout this text the word Mitsrayim will be used in place of the English word Egypt since

that is how it is rendered in the Torah.

⁹ Ya'akov is a proper transliteration for the name which is often called Jacob in English, the same name as the patriarch whose name was changed to Yisra'el and who fathered the Tribes of Yisra'el. It is also the correct Hebrew name for the Disciple traditionally called James.

¹⁰ See Numbers (Bemidbar) 2:1 - 2:34. The Torah speaks extensively about the stranger, the guest, the foreigner and the sojourner often called the ger (גר) and the towshab (חושב) and continuously makes provision for them. There were always strangers and sojourners living with Yisra'el and one of the primary purposes of Yisra'el besides their ministry to YHWH was their ministry to the stranger, not only to point them to YHWH but to incorporate them into the Nation if the person desired to do so and was willing to obey the Commandments. This topic is described in much greater detail in the Walk in the Light Series book entitled "The Redeemed" and it is critical to understand this issue to avoid the false doctrine of Replacement Theology and other beliefs which continually separate and divide Believers into categories such as "Jews" and "Gentiles". A Gentile was someone outside the Assembly of Yisra'el, often called a heathen. If and when a person becomes one of the Redeemed, they are grafted into Yisra'el and it is no longer appropriate to refer them as a Gentile. Likewise, even if a person is a genetic descendent of Ya'akov, and call themselves a "Jew" they are not a part of Yisra'el unless they are one of the Redeemed and obey the Torah. The Messiah came to unite, not divide His Assembly into subcategories based upon genetic heritage.

¹¹ The words "Jewish", "Jews" and "Jew" are in italics because they are ambiguous and sometimes derogatory and misleading terms. In modern day, these expressions are sometimes used to describe all of the genetic descendants of Ya'akov while at other times the words describe adherents to the religion of Judaism. The terms are commonly applied to ancient Yisra'elites as well as modern day descendents of those tribes, whether they are atheists, Orthodox, Messianic, Christian etc. In other words, the word has become secularized and often has nothing to do with a person's spiritual condition and is solely based upon their

genetic lineage. This is exactly the opposite of what it meant to be a Yisra'elite which depended upon your obedience and submission to the Elohim of Yisra'el, YHWH, and had nothing to do with genetics. Anybody could join Yisra'el if they demonstrated their faith in YHWH by obeying His commandments. The word "Jew" originally referred to a member of the tribe of Judah (Yahudah) or a person that lived in the region of Judea. After the different exiles of the House of Yisra'el and the House of Yahudah, it was the Yahudim that returned to the land while the House of Yisra'el was scattered to the ends of the earth (Yirmeyahu 9:16). Since the Yahudim represented the recognizable descendents of Ya'akov, they came to represent Yisra'el and over time, with the Kingdom of Yisra'el in exile, the Yahudim came to represent Yisra'el and thus the term "Jew" was used to describe a Yisra'elite. While this label became common and customary, it is not accurate and is the cause of tremendous confusion. This subject is described in greater detail in The Walk in the Light Series book entitled "The Redeemed".

[12] Jamieson, Fausset, and Brown Commentary.

[13] Yeshayahu (ישעיהו) is the proper transliteration for the prophet commonly called Isaiah. His name means: "Yah saves". Yah being the poetic short form of the Name of YHWH.

[14] The correct Hebrew Name for the Messiah commonly called Jesus, is Yahushua (יהושע). It is the same Name as the Hebrew Patriarch commonly called Joshua and it means "Yah is salvation". This subject is discussed in detail in The Walk in the Light Series book entitled "Names".

[15] The proper description of the place where YHWH dwells is The House of YHWH or rather Beit HaMikdash, The Set Apart House. Nowhere in the Torah will you find the word "temple". In fact, the House of YHWH is only called a Temple in certain translations after Solomon built the his House on Mt. Moriah. The word which is often translated as "temple" is beit (בית) which simply means "house". Since temple is so often associated with the place where pagans worship their deities I prefer to avoid the word if and when possible.

[16] Yahonatan is a transliteration for the name of the disciple often called Jonathan or John. His name means "Yah is gracious".

17   I refer to Yahushua using a form of the Hebrew word mashiach (מָשִׁיחַ) which is translated Messiah and means "anointed". When you refer to Yahushua as The Messiah, there is no question what you mean, especially of the context of the Hebrew Scriptures. The word "christ" is a Greek term which also means "anointed" but is applied to any number of their pagan gods. Therefore, the title Messiah seems more appropriate when referring to the Hebrew Messiah.

18   The proper Hebrew transliteration for the City commonly called Jerusalem is Yahrushalayim (יְרוּשָׁלַם). There is no "j" sound in Hebrew and most of the time when you see an English spelling with a "j" it should be a "y" sound.

19   According to the UMJC website: "Criteria for chartering Messianic Jewish congregations, fellowships and non-congregational ministries: 2. The applying congregation shall have at least 10 Messianic Jewish members* (By definition, a Messianic Jew is a Jewish person who has repented and received Messiah Yeshua as his or her own personal atonement.)" See www.umjc.org/main/docs/standards.aspx. I personally find this to be disquieting because it continues the erroneous and divisive policy of separating Believers based upon genetics. If an assembly has less than 10 genetically "Jewish" converts then they cannot join the Union of Messianic Jewish Congregations. Where they came up with 10 one can only speculate but it appears that it comes from the Rabbinic Jewish tradition of requiring a minion (also minyan) of 10 or more persons for the recitation of daily or Sabbath prayers. This is modified Rabbinic Judaism and separates and divides rather than restoring and unifying the Assembly. The implication is that a gathering for prayer is only legitimate if there are 10 "Jews" present. While I can understand the UMJC's desire to unite and encourage Believing "Jews", their exclusionary policies may end up doing damage in the end by separating the Body of Messiah just as denominations have done in Christianity.

20   The moadim are discussed in more detail in the Walk in the Light Series book entitled "Appointed Times".

21   A detailed discussion of the identity of the Redeemed of
YHWH can be found in the Walk in the Light Series book
entitled "The Redeemed". One of the greatest tragedies
perpetrated by Christianity is a doctrine known as Replacement
Theology which teaches that Christians have replaced Yisra'el.
This is simply not true as can be seen by a close examination of
the first Believers who were Hebrews that remained
Yisra'elites. They did not "convert" to Christianity when they
believed in Yahushua, they actually became a sect of Yisra'elites
called The Way, among various other labels.

22   The renewed covenant, often called the "New Covenant" is not
really so new. In fact, you must look in the Tanakh to find the
terms of this covenant which are set forth by the Prophet
Yirmeyahu as follows: "*[31] The time is coming, declares YHWH,
"when I will make a renewed covenant with the house of Yisra'el and
with the house of Yahudah. [32] It will not be like the covenant I made
with their forefathers when I took them by the hand to lead them out
of Mitsrayim, because they broke my covenant, though I was a
husband to them," declares YHWH. [33] This is the covenant I will
make with the house of Yisra'el after that time, declares YHWH. I
will put my Torah in their minds and write it on their hearts. I
will be their Elohim, and they will be my people. [34] No longer will a
man teach his neighbor or a man his brother, saying, Know YHWH,
because they will all know me, from the least of them to the greatest,
declares YHWH. For I will forgive their wickedness and will
remember their sins no more.*" Yirmeyahu 31:31-34. The Hebrew
word often translated as "New" is chadash (חדשה) which
means "fresh" or "renewed". This covenant is made with
Yisra'el, not "The Church". The covenants found within the
Scriptures are dealt with at length in the Walk in the Light
Series book entitled "Covenants".

23   Mattityahu is the proper translation for the name of the disciple
commonly called Matthew. His name means: "Gift of Yah".

24   This Scripture confounds Christians for a couple different
reasons. First, it instructs them to pray that there flight does
not occur on a day that they do not even observe. Second it
talks about them fleeing tribulation when many believe they are
going to be "raptured" before their feathers get ruffled. The
false doctrine of the pre-tribulation rapture is discussed in

greater detail in the Walk in the Light Series book entitled
"The Final Shofar".

25 While much of the world calculates the beginning of a new day
after midnight, the Scriptural day begins after sunset. This is
why people often have trouble understanding certain
occurrences such as the resurrection of the Messiah on Shabbat
rather than Sunday.

26 This is the difference between practicing a religion and obeying
the Torah. Rabbinic Judaism has created extensive prayers and
traditions for every aspect of life. While some of these may be
useful and instructive they may also create burdens upon
adherents similar to those described by the Messiah when He
rebuked the Pharisees. (Luke 11:46). It is always important to
remember the simplicity of the Torah and the fact that it is not
too hard to obey the commandments (Devarim 30:11) although
men often make it impossible.

27 All of the moadim found in Vayiqra 23 are rehearsals which are
intended to teach us the plan of YHWH and help us prepare
for the coming of the Messiah. We are continually instructed in
the Scriptures to watch and pray. If you understand and
observe the Appointed Times you will know what to watch for
and you will be prepared for His coming.

28 In this modern day we use books in codex form which are
bound by a spine and generally have writing on both pages. By
using the word "book" we create a mental image regarding
manuscripts which may not be accurate. Manuscripts such as
the Torah and other writings in the Tanakh were written on
scrolls, so instead of the word book, it is more accurate to refer
to the scroll or the sefer (ספר) when referring to these ancient
manuscripts.

29 Nehemyah is the proper transliteration for the name commonly
spelled Nehemiah which means: "Yah consoles" or "comforted
of Yah".

30 The Feast of Succot occurs in what is commonly referred to as
the Fall, although the Land of Yisra'el only has two seasons,
summer and winter. This is where we have the distinction
between the former and the later rains. The former rains occur
during the summer harvest and consists of the barley harvest
during the month of the aviv (אבב) which coincides with

pesach (Passover) and the wheat harvest during Shavuot (Pentecost). The later harvest includes grapes and figs among other things and people would bring their new wine, their grapes and figs to Yahrushalayim as their firstfruit offerings during the Feast of Succot. All of these moadim and the crops associated with them are important in understanding the Scriptures and prophesies concerning the coming days. These issues are discussed in depth in the Walk in the Light Series book entitled "Appointed Times".

[31] A discussion on the timing of the crucifixion and resurrection of Yahushua topic is discussed in the Walk in the Light Series book entitled "Appointed Times" as well as the Walk in the Light Series book entitled "Pagan Holidays".

[32] Synagogue is a Greek translation of the Hebrew Beit K'nesset (House of Assembly) which some find very cold. Some prefer to use the word shul which is Yiddish and derives from the German word for school and emphasizes the study which takes place therein. "The Orthodox and Chasidim typically use the word "shul" while Conservative Jews usually use the word "synagogue," which is actually a Greek translation of Beit K'nesset and means "place of assembly" (it's related to the word "synod"). Reform Jews use the word "temple," because they consider every one of their meeting places to be equivalent to, or a replacement for, The Temple." www.shomairyisrael.org.

[33] Many modern English translations use the phrase "Lord of the Sabbath." The Greek word which is often translated lord is kurios (κυριοσ) which means "one in supreme authority, a master, lord". Due to the overuse of the word "lord", its improper replacement of the True Name of the Creator and its relationship with Baal worship, I prefer to use the term Master. For a more detailed discussion of the use of the word "lord" in the Scriptures see the Walk in the Light Series book entitled "Names".

[34] Kepha is the proper transliteration for the name of the disciple commonly called Peter.

[35] Modern calculations using computer generated models have determined the actual birth date of the Messiah to be September 23, 3 B.C.E. on the Gregorian Calendar which was

Tishri 15, 3998 according to the Scriptural Calendar. This date is confirmed by the Scriptures and the month of Tishri is the seventh month of the Scriptural year. For more information on the birth of Yahushua see the Walk in the Light Series book entitled "Appointed Times".

[36] The Seventh month contains the Appointed Times commonly referred to as "the Fall Feasts". These appointed times include the Day of Trumpets, The Day of Atonement and Succot (The Feast of Tabernacles). These are shadow pictures or rehearsals of things to come and they will include the return of the Messiah, Judgment, and Him dwelling (tabernacling) with His people. The prophet Zekaryah states that Succot will be observed from year to year throughout the millennial reign. (Zekaryah 14:16). These Appointed Times are discussed in more detail in the Walk in the Light Series book entitled "Appointed Times".

[37] See Zekaryah 14:9; Yeshayahu 24:23; Daniel 2:44; Revelation 11:15.

[38] The Jewish Book of Why, Alfred J. Kolatch, Penguin Group (2000) p.173.

[39] Some believe that as a result of this passage, the Gentile converts were only required to obey four specific commandments; but that is clearly not the intent of the passage. The Yahrushalayim Council met to discuss how to deal with the influx of Gentiles who were converting to the faith, which, after salvation through grace, required righteous living in accordance with the Torah. Since the Torah was most likely foreign to the pagans coming into the faith, the Elders provided some initial guidance with the assumption that the converts would observe the Sabbath, attend synagogue and hear, learn and obey the Torah. This subject is discussed at length in The Walk in the Light Series book entitled "The Law and Grace".

[40] Yirmeyahu is the proper transliteration for the prophet commonly called Jeremiah. His name means: "Yah will lift up or exalt".

[41] Shaul (sha ool) is the proper transliteration for the name of the apostle commonly called Paul.

[42] The Scriptures, Institute for Scripture Research (1998) Page 1164.

[43] Jewish New Testament Commentary, David H. Stern, Jewish

New Testament Publications, Inc., 1992, Page 434.

[44] *A Commentary on the Jewish Roots of Romans*, Joseph Shulam, Messianic Jewish Publishers, 1997, Page 461.

[45] *Divine Rest for Human Restlessness*, Appendix - From Sabbath to Sunday, Dr. Samuele Bacchiocchi, Biblical Perspectives 2002.

[46] A review of Christian history reveals that many unscriptural events and teachings have come out of Antioch. Therefore the actions and teachings of believers in that city are not necessarily to be condoned just because they happened hundreds of years ago. One of the most eloquent leaders of early Christendom, Bishop John Chrysostom "The Golden Mouthed" came out of Antioch. He was a blatant anti-semite and gave eight sermons under the title "Against the Jews." It appears that many of the practices and edicts which came out of Antioch were intended to separate the Gentile Converts from their Hebrew brethren. Therefore the fact that they first called themselves "Christians" in Antioch is not necessarily a positive statement or an endorsement of the title "Christian" especially in light of the fact that "Christ" is not a Hebrew word and was often used by pagans to refer to their deities. It is important to understand the powerful effect that the Greco-Roman culture had on early Christianity, especially within the early assembly. One would think that since they were closer in time to the physical ministry of the Messiah that they would have a purer doctrine, untainted from the many false doctrines which have permeated the religion over the centuries, but this is simply not so. Many of the early Believers were former pagans who lived in a Hellenistic society which often influenced their actions and thinking. It is important to remember that these people were human and subject to evil influences just as much as Believers today. It is therefore important to test things whether they were written yesterday or two thousand years ago.

[47] *Forerunners and Rivals of Christianity*, Legge, pp. 132-133.

[48] *Come Out of Her My People*, Koster, C.J., Institute for Scripture Research (1998) p. 16.

[49] *The Story of Christian Theology*, Roger E. Olson, InterVarsity Press 1999, p. 138.

[50] *Come Out of Her My People* at p. 14.

[51] A. de A. Paiva, O Mitraismo, p. 3.

The word "church" is a man-made word typically associated with the Catholic and Christian religions. In that context it is meant to describe the corporate body of faith. It is used in most modern English Bibles as a translation for the Greek word ekklesia (εκκλεσια) which simply means "assembly". It does not necessarily have any religious connotation as can be seen in Acts 19:39-41 where the word ekklesia was used to refer to the courts and also the riotous mob that was accusing some of the disciples. When applied to Believers it refers to the "called out assembly of YHWH." The word "church" derives from pagan origins and its misuse is part of the problem associated with Replacement Theology which teaches that the "Church" has replaced Yisra'el, which in Hebrew is called the qahal (קהל): "the called out assembly of YHWH." The Hebrew *qahal* and Greek *ekklesia* therefore represent the same thing when referring to Believers: The Commonwealth of Yisra'el. Therefore, the continued use of the word "church" is divisive, confusing and simply incorrect. This subject is described in grated detail in The Walk in the Light Series book entitled "The Redeemed".

53 *The Converts Catechism of Catholic Doctrine*, Peter Geiermann, C.S.S.R., (1957), p. 50.

54 *The Faith of our Fathers*, James Cardinal Gibbons, 88th ed., p. 89.

55 *The Catholic Record*, London, Ontario, Canada, September 1, 1923.

56 *Catholic Press*, Sydney Australia, August 1900.

57 *A Doctrinal Catechism*, Stephan Keenan, 1846 edition, p. 176.

58 Priest Brady address at Elizabeth, N.J. on March 17, 1903, reported in Elizabeth, N.J. News, March 18, 1903.

59 Catholic Church Extension Society, Peter R. Kraemer Chicago, Illinois (1975).

60 Priest F.G. Lentz, The Question Box, 1900, p. 98.

61 A "jot" is commonly defined as an "iota" (i) which is the smallest letter in the Greek alphabet or the dot on an "i". A "tittle" is commonly referred to as a "stroke" or the apex of a Hebrew letter. Since Yahushua was not talking about Greek or English, but rather Hebrew, it is important to understand what "jots" and "tittles" mean in the Hebrew context. Torah scrolls are meticulously copied by Scribes and include, not only

Hebrew letters, but also dots, markings and spaces as well as enlarged, reduced and inverted letters which were made by Mosheh. These "jots" and "tittles" all have meaning beyond the actual Hebrew text, but you will only find them in the Hebrew Scriptures.

62 *The Christian Baptist*, Alexander Campbell, Feb. 2, 1824, vol. 1. no. 7, p. 164.

63 *Sabbath or Sunday*, John Theodore Mueller, pp. 15, 16.

64 John Wesley, The Works of the Rev. John Wesley, A.M., John Emory, ed. (New York: Eaton & Mains), Sermon 25, vol. 1, p. 221.

65 *Weighed and Wanting*, D.L. Moody, (Fleming H. Revell Co.: New York), pp. 47-48.

66 *Theology Condensed*, T.C. Blake, D.D., pp. 474-475.

67 *The Ten Commandments*, Dr. R. W. Dale, Hodderand Stoughton, page 106-107.

68 *Keeping the Sabbath – A Healthy Habit*, Clifford Bajema, The Banner, CRC Publications 2005.

69 Yehezqel is the proper transliteration for the prophet commonly called Ezekiel. His name means: "El will strengthen". El is the short form of Elohim.

70 The argument that obedience to the Torah is placing a person under bondage is misleading. On numerous occasions the disciples called themselves bondservants. (Romans 1:1; Ya'akov 1:1; 2 Kepha 1:1; Yahudah 1). A bondservant has a Master and a bondservant obeys their Master. It is as simple as that. If you have been redeemed, saved by grace, then your reasonable service involves being set apart through obedience. (Romans 12:1). You are not free to do anything that you want, especially not those things which are clearly displeasing to your Master. On the contrary, you derive pleasure from obeying your Master which, in turn, gives Him pleasure. The beauty of this process is that with YHWH as your Master you are richly blessed for your obedience. There is a distinct difference between a slave and a bondservant. A slave is forced to obey, a bondservant willingly obeys. You are free to choose with YHWH, but once you have chosen you must do it His way which is the best way.

71 It is important to reemphasize so that there is no confusion: "For it is by grace you have been saved, through faith, and this

not from yourselves, it is the gift of Elohim - not by works, so that no one can boast." Ephesians 2:8-9. The gift is the redemption that we receive through the blood of Yahushua which cleanses us from our transgressions. (Romans 3:20-26). The important point to remember is you were once under the penalty of death because you transgressed the commandments. Once you have been cleansed, you need to stop transgressing the commandments and start obeying. This does not place you "under the law" it sets you on the path of righteousness. The Torah define righteous and unrighteous conduct so it is imperative to know and follow the Torah through the help of the Spirit (Ruach) in order to walk the straight and true path of righteousness.

72 *Natural Cures "They" Don't Want You To Know About*, Kevin Trudeau, Alliance Publishing Group, Inc. 2004, p. 139.

Appendix A

The Lunar Sabbath

Many that begin to understand and observe the Sabbath will run across certain arguments concerning the Lunar Sabbath. Briefly, adherents to this notion believe that the Sabbath count is dictated by the lunar cycle. According to the Lunar Sabbath model, when a New Moon is sighted it begins the Sabbath count and the cycle of Sabbaths which will occur on the Eighth, Fifteenth, Twenty Second and Twenty Ninth days. If no new moon is sighted on the Thirtieth day, then that day would merge with the Twenty Ninth day as a Sabbath and according to some, the day of the sighting also becomes a Sabbath.

Based upon my calculations using the Lunar Sabbath model there will be times when there are back to back Sabbaths, sometimes three Sabbath days in a row. This seems a bit odd and inconsistent with the seventh day Sabbath cycle which has been observed consistently around the globe for thousands of years (ie. six days of work followed by one day of rest).

For those who are unfamiliar with the significance of the New Moon, this may seem to be an apparent error. The importance of the New Moon as it relates to YHWH's calendar is discussed at length in the Walk in the Light Series book entitled "Appointed Times". Suffice it to say, it is a very important subject and historically New Moons have been treated as special and with celebration. Therefore, the Lunar Sabbath is not to be hastily disregarded.

In fact, certain Scriptures have linked the New Moons and Sabbaths together. For instance: *"On the Sabbaths and New Moons the people of the land are to worship* in the presence of YHWH at the entrance to that gateway." Yehezqel 46:3. Also we read: "It will be the duty of the prince to provide the burnt offerings, grain offerings and drink offerings at the festivals, the New Moons and the Sabbaths-at all the appointed feasts of the house of Yisrael." Yehezqel 45:17. There are several other passages which group the Sabbaths, New Moons and feasts together in the general category of appointed times. The important thing to realize is that these appointed times are in different categories and thus unique. The Sabbath is separate from a feast and the same holds true concerning the New Moons.

Now some Lunar Sabbath adherents state that the New Moons are not the same as Sabbaths, they merely start the Sabbath count. They find support for this proposition in Tehillim 104:19 which states: "He appointed the moon for seasons; the sun knows its' going down." NKJV. In the Hebrew this verse literally says that He appointed the moon for "moadim". In other words, the moon determines the timing of the moadim, that would not include the Sabbath which is a uniquely special day that began its count during the first week of creation which was not based upon the newly created moon.

During the first week of creation the sun and the moon were created on the fourth day (Beresheet 1:14-19). We are not told what phase the moon was in on the fourth day but since YHWH calls the crescent moon the New Moon, or rather "Rosh Chodesh" which literally means "Head of the Month" it is safe to say that it was either 1) a new crescent moon or 2) in the fourth day of the lunar phase since the first month began three days prior to that time.

The first scenario does not support the lunar Sabbath model. While the second scenario would be consistent with the lunar Sabbath for the first month, it would soon deviate. In short, there is no indication from the Scriptures that the Sabbath count was reset each New Moon or had any direct relation to the Lunar Cycle.

Rather it appears undisputed that the seven day week, with the seventh day Sabbath, continues to this day as a testament to creation. In my opinion the Lunar Sabbath model is very confusing and burdensome and though interesting, it is not supported by the Scriptures.

Appendix B

The Continuous Sabbath Cycle

A question which is often posed by people who begin to understand the current relevance and significance of the Sabbath is: How do we know that the day we commonly call Saturday is still the seventh day? In other words, they want to know whether the seven day week cycle has remained uninterrupted since creation assuring that the seventh day we recognize today as the Sabbath is actually the seventh day.

There is no underlying historical argument to suggest that there has ever been any change in the Sabbath cycle so this is really nothing more than an interesting question. Regardless, it is a valid question with an easy answer but a somewhat complicated explanation. First, the answer is that the Sabbath which is universally recognized today is, in fact, the seventh day.

Historians and astronomers all seem to agree that there has been no interruption of the weekly cycle during any period of recorded history. For those who believe in the accuracy of the Scriptures this would lead to the conclusion that there has been no interruption in the weekly cycle since the first week of creation. Astro-Archaeology, a field which uses historical records combined with computer models, can confirm through known solar and lunar eclipses that the days of the week have remained the same over the millennia. It does this by comparing historical records which provide dates and accounts of eclipses and then confirms them with our present day calendar via computer programs. This technique has validated the present day calendar.

Some believe that the change from the Julian calendar to the Gregorian Calendar affected the weekly cycle but that is not correct. In 1582 an error in the Julian Calendar was corrected by implementing the Gregorian Calendar. Under the Julian Calendar a year was reckoned as 365.25 solar days long although a solar year should have actually been calculated as 365.242195 days in length. Over the centuries what originally was a very small discrepancy resulted in a shift of 10 days. Between the years 1582 and 1752, various countries throughout the world adopted the Gregorian Calendar which resynchronized the date, but never impacted the day of the week. In other words, when countries implemented the Gregorian Calendar, they changed the number of the date of a month, but not the day of the week.

Finally, there have always been a remnant of Torah observant Believers throughout history who have maintained not only the accuracy of the Scriptures, but also the accuracy of the Sabbath day. As far as I know none of these groups have ever claimed that the Sabbath has shifted at any time in history. Therefore, based upon all of this evidence it is my opinion that we can "rest assured" that the Sabbath that we recognize as beginning of Friday at sundown and ending on Saturday at sundown is, in fact, the seventh day Sabbath.

Appendix C

The Walk in the Light Series

Book 1   Restoration – A discussion of the pagan influences that have mixed with the true faith through the ages which has resulted in the need for restoration. This book also examines true Scriptural restoration.

Book 2   Names – Discusses the True Name of the Creator and the Messiah as well as the significance of names in the Scriptures.

Book 3   Scriptures – Discusses the origin of the written Scriptures as well as many translation errors which have led to false doctrines in some mainline religions.

Book 4   Covenants – Discusses the progressive covenants between the Creator and His Creation as described in the Scriptures which reveals His plan for mankind.

Book 5   The Messiah – Discusses the prophetic promises and fulfillments of the Messiah and the True identity of the Redeemer of Yisra'el.

Book 6   The Redeemed – Discusses the relationship between Christianity and Judaism and details how the Scriptures identify True Believers. It reveals how the Christian doctrine of Replacement Theology has caused confusion as to how the Creator views the Children of Yisra'el.

Book 7   Law and Grace – Discusses in depth the false doctrine that Grace has done away with the Law and demonstrates the vital importance of obeying the commandments.

Book 8   The Sabbath – Discusses the importance of the Seventh Day Sabbath as well as the origins of the tradition concerning Sunday worship.

Book 9   Kosher – Discusses the importance of eating food prescribed by the Scriptures as a aspect of righteous living.

Book 10   Appointed Times – Discusses the appointed times established by the Creator, often erroneously considered to be "Jewish" holidays, and critical to the understanding of prophetic fulfillment of the Scriptural promises.

Book 11   Pagan Holidays – Discusses the pagan origins of some popular Christian holidays which have replaced the Appointed Times.

Book 12   The Final Shofar – Discusses the walk required by the Scriptures and prepares the Believer for the deceptions coming in the End of Days.

The series began as a simple Powerpoint presentation which was intended to develop into a book with twelve different chapters but ended up being twelve different books. Each book is intended to stand alone although the series was originally intended to build from one section to another. Due to the urgency of certain topics, the books have not been published in sequential order.

For anticipated release dates, announcements and additional teachings go to:
www.shemayisrael.net

Appendix D

The Shema

Deuteronomy (Devarim) 6:4-5

Hear, O Israel: The LORD our God, the LORD is one!
You shall love the LORD your God with all your heart,
with all your soul, and with all your strength.

Traditional English Translation

שמע ישראל יהוה אלהינו יהוה אחד ואהבה
את יהוה אלהיך בכל־ לבבך ובכל־ נפשך ובכל־ מאדך

Hebrew Text

Shema, Yisra'el: YHWH Elohenu, YHWH echad!
V-ahavta et YHWH Elohecha b-chol l'vavcha u-v-chol
naf'sh'cha u-v-chol m'odecha.

Hebrew Text Transliterated